10 Minute Guide
to System 7

Harry McQuillen IV

SAMS

A Division of Macmillan Computer Publishing

11711 North College, Carmel, Indiana 46032 USA

*To my family, friends, and Erin, my dog, all of whom helped
me through this book*

FIRST EDITION
SECOND PRINTING—1991

International Standard Book Number: 0-672-30033-8
Library of Congress Catalog Card Number: 91-62685

Publisher: *Richard K. Swadley*
Associate Publisher: *Marie Butler-Knight*
Managing Editor: *Marjorie Hopper*
Acquisitions and Development Editor: *Stephen R. Poland*
Technical Editor: *Stephen R. Poland*
Network Technical Consultant: *Bill Trenchard*
Manuscript Editor: *Charles A. Hutchinson*
Cover Design: *Dan Armstrong*
Designer: *Scott Cook*
Indexer: *Hilary Adams*
Production: *Mike Britton, Scott Boucher, Brad Chinn, Martin Coleman, Joelynn Gifford, Debbie Hanna, David McKenna, Matthew Morrill, Mary Beth Wakefield, Corinne Walls, Jenny Watson*

Printed in the United States of America.

Contents

Introduction

In the past, Macintosh users most often used the system software that came with their computer. The system software that you have on your Macintosh is probably some version of System 6. Apple Computer has released a new version of the system software called System 7. It offers improvements over System 6 and many new features. You've probably heard something about this new system and have bought it from your Apple dealer or maybe your office is upgrading to System 7.

Welcome to the *10 Minute Guide to System 7*.

Because most people don't have the luxury of sitting down uninterrupted for hours at a time to learn a new program or system and because you already have experience with the basic Macintosh functions, the *10 Minute Guide to System 7* teaches only the new features you need and the changes from System 6 in lessons that you can complete in 10 minutes or less. Not only does the 10-minute format offer information in bite-sized, easy-to-follow modules, it lets you stop and start as often as you like because each lesson is a self-contained series of steps related to a particular task.

What Is the *10 Minute Guide*?

The *10 Minute Guide* is a new approach to learning computer programs. Instead of trying to teach you *everything* about a particular software product, the *10 Minute Guide* teaches you only about the most often-used features. Each *10 Minute Guide* contains between 20 and 30 short lessons.

The *10 Minute Guide* teaches you about programs and systems without relying on computerese or technical jargon—you'll find only simple English used to explain the procedures in this book. With straightforward, easy-to-follow steps and special artwork called icons to call your attention to important tips and definitions, the *10 Minute Guide* makes learning a new software program quick and easy.

The following icons help you find your way around in the *10 Minute Guide to System 7*:

Timesaver Tips offer shortcuts and hints for using the program more effectively.

Plain English icons appear when new terms are defined.

Panic Button icons identify problem areas and how to solve them.

Additionally, a "System Software Primer" is included at the back of the book to explain the basic Macintosh functions if you are unsure of your ability to use a Macintosh or have let your skills fall into disuse.

Specific conventions are used to help find your way around System 7 as easily as possible.

Numbered steps	Step-by-step instructions are highlighted so that you can easily find the procedures you need to perform basic System 7 operations.
Selections	The names of menus, buttons, and menu selections are shown in bold color for easy recognition.

The *10 Minute Guide to System 7* is organized in 20 lessons, ranging from basic installation information to more advanced printing and inter-application communication features. Remember, however, that nothing in this book is difficult. Most users want to start at the first lesson and progress sequentially (unless you first review the primer).

For Further Reference...

SAMS publishes several other books that will help increase your knowledge of System 7 after you've completed this *10 Minute Guide*:

The First Book of the Mac

10 Minute Guide to the Mac

Trademarks

All terms mentioned in this book that are known to be trademarks or service marks are listed below. In addition, terms suspected of being trademarks or service marks have been appropriately capitalized. SAMS cannot attest to the accuracy of this information. Use of a term in this book should not be regarded as affecting the validity of any trademark or service mark.

Apple, Macintosh, AppleTalk, and LaserWriter are registered trademarks of Apple Computer, Inc. Macintosh IIsi, IIci, IIfx, SE/30, 512k, and Macintosh Plus are also registered trademarks of Apple Computer, Inc.

CompuServe is a registered trademark of CompuServe Incorporated and H&R Block.

Norton Utilities is a registered trademark of Peter Norton Computing.

PostScript is a registered trademark of Adobe Systems Incorporated.

Other product and service names are trademarks and service marks of their respective owners.

Lessons

Lesson 1
What Is
System 7?

In this lesson you'll learn the basics of System 7.

What Is System 7?

System 7 is a new release of the operating system for Macintosh computers. System 7 is an improvement over the previous versions of the system (5 and 6 most recently) because it provides new features that make the Macintosh more powerful and easier to use. Following is a brief list of some of these features and what they do:

- *File sharing*—Lets you easily use folders and files from other users' computers on a network.

- *New Find built into the Finder*—Lets you find items on your hard disk quickly and easily.

- *New System folder arrangement*—Ends bulky and unmanageable System folders.

- *Aliasing*—Lets you easily open files and applications from anywhere on your computer, even from the Apple menu.

- *New control panels*—Let you easily set options in your computer.

- *Publish and Subscribe*—A "live" copy-and-paste feature that automatically updates information whenever it is changed.

- *New 3-D look*—Changes appearance of the windows and icons for quick recognition.

- *Balloon Help*—Provides a better system for getting help with the Finder and many applications.

Where To Get System 7

Starting in August, 1991, all new Macintosh computers will be shipped with System 7. But more than likely, you already have a Macintosh and want to use the new system. It is available from a number of sources, the most well known being Apple Computer. Apple has two upgrade kits. The first, the Personal Upgrade Kit, contains

- System 7 disks on 800K floppy disks

- Networking Basics disk

- Before You Install disk

- HyperCard 2.1

- Full set of replacement manuals for your Macintosh

The Apple Personal Upgrade Kit is available from your local Apple dealer and many software retailers. It has a list price of $99.

If you use your Macintosh at home or do not work on a network, then the Personal Upgrade Kit is probably the best way to upgrade. If, however, your company uses multiple Macintoshes and/or has a network, the Group Upgrade Kit may be the best option. The Group Upgrade Kit contains a CD-ROM disk, which has the capability to update all Macs on a network and make as many sets of system disks as needed. Check with your computer support staff for information about group upgrading.

You also can obtain System 7 from local users' groups. These groups may charge a small copying fee for System 7, and supplying your own disks is generally a good idea. Users' group upgrades come with either no documentation or electronic documentation. So check with your users' group for more information.

To get information about users' groups... Apple Computer maintains a toll-free number (1-800-538-9696) that you can call for information on local users' groups.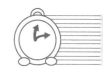

If you have a modem, you also can obtain System 7 electronically. It is available on large commercial services like GEnie, CompuServe, and America Online. In addition, many computer Bulletin Board Systems (BBSs) are authorized by Apple to distribute System 7 through a modem. You can obtain numbers of local BBSs from local users' groups, or you can get BBS lists from large networks like America Online, CompuServe, or GEnie.

BBS A Bulletin Board System is a service, operated by an individual or users' group, which provides a basic structure for exchanging files and messages using a modem.

Hardware Requirements

System 7 requires at least 2M (2 megabytes) of RAM and a hard disk drive. To use System 7 to its best possible advantage, you may require larger amounts of memory. Table 1-1 shows the suggested memory needed to run the system.

Table 1-1. Memory requirements for System 7.

Computer	Suggested Memory	Format
Mac 128k, 512k, 512ke	2-4 megabytes	Third party upgrade
Mac Classic, Portable	2-4 megabytes	Expansion board
Mac Plus, SE,	2-4 megabytes	4 SIMM slots
Mac LC, IIsi	4-8 megabytes	2 SIMM slots
Mac II, IIx, IIcx, IIci, IIfx, SE/30	4-8 megabytes	8 SIMM slots

There are several ways to obtain more memory if you don't have the required memory for System 7. Using SIMMs is the easiest way to expand your memory if you can support them (see the "Format" column of Table 1-1). SIMMs are available in ¼M (256K), 1M, 2M, and 4M options. In Macintosh II machines, you must install the SIMMs in sets of four; in all other Macintoshes you must install SIMMs in sets of two.

SIMM SIMM is an acronym for Single In-line Memory Module. A SIMM is a circuit board with memory already soldered onto it, so you don't have to deal with the individual chips.

Apple Computer sells SIMMs through their dealers in Apple Memory Upgrade Kits. While these kits are easy to install (your dealer will install them for you), they are expensive. You also can buy SIMMs from third party retailers. Many of the larger mail order companies like MacWarehouse and MacConnection offer detailed instructions and even videotapes that tell you how to install your SIMMs.

Installing SIMMs yourself By installing SIMMs yourself, you can void the warranty of your Mac Plus, SE, Classic, or SE/30, and you can short-circuit your computer if you don't take proper antistatic precautions. Also, you need a special tool kit to open these machines to install memory. Many retailers offer kits to open your Mac and protect your computer from static.

Portable and Classic owners must get an expansion board to install more memory. Apple offers both of these boards, and third party retailers offer options that allow you to use SIMMs in these machines.

If you have one of the older Macintoshes (128k, 512k, 512ke), expanding the memory isn't as easy. To upgrade your computer to use System 7, you need to purchase a third party upgrade board that has both memory expansion and a Small Computer System Interface (SCSI) port. The SCSI port enables you to use a hard drive on your computer. Also, you might want to take this opportunity to speed up your aging Mac with an accelerator card. Accelerator cards make your applications run faster, increasing your productivity.

5

This lesson has explained what System 7 is and the requirements for using it. The next lesson will show you how to prepare your system before installing System 7.

Lesson 2
Before You Upgrade to System 7

In this lesson you'll learn what to do before you install System 7.

Before you install System 7, you should make a backup of your files and check your current files to see if they're compatible with System 7.

Backing Up

Apple suggests that you make a backup of your hard disk drive before installing System 7 because the upgrade process could damage your files. Following are two ways to back up your disk:

- *Commercial backup programs*—There are quite a few commercial backup programs available, and any one of these (such as Retrospect and Fastback) enables you to back up any part of your hard drive to floppy disks or tapes.

7

- *Manual backup*—It's less expensive (but more work) to back up manually. You should copy all nonreplaceable files (applications can be reinstalled from original disks in case of an emergency) to floppy disks and store them in a safe place until you're sure that everything went well with the installation. In fact, it's a good idea to have a backup of **all** important files.

Compatibility Checker

The Before You Install System 7 disk comes with the upgrade kit from Apple. The kit consists of two HyperCard stacks. The first stack is called BYI (Before You Install) and contains general information about upgrading to System 7. Here you will look at the second stack, the Compatibility Checker, which checks your hard disk drive and finds applications and files that will work or will not work well with System 7. For the applications that aren't System 7 compatible, the Compatibility Checker recommends newer versions or alternatives.

1. Make sure that HyperCard version 1.2.2 or newer is on your hard drive. If it is not, copy HyperCard and the Home stack from the HyperCard program disk, which came with your upgrade.

2. Insert the Before You Install System 7 disk and double-click on the Compatibility Checker stack (see Figure 2-1).

3. If you have more than one hard drive installed on your system, click on Set Up at the first card to begin the process. The screen will clear, and the next card will be visible (see Figure 2-2). If you have only one hard drive on your system, skip to step 5.

Figure 2-1. The Compatibility Checker icon.

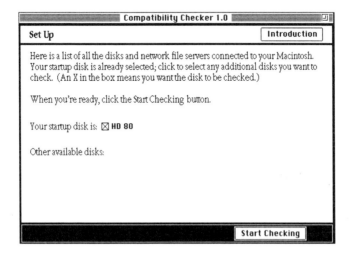

Figure 2-2. The Setup screen.

4. On the lower portion of the screen there is a series of check boxes representing all the disks on-line. Check all of the boxes corresponding to the disks you want to have the Compatibility Checker look over.

5. Click **Start Checking**.

As the Compatibility Checker scans your hard drive(s), a progress bar shows you how the scan is progressing. When the scan is finished, a window is displayed listing the items in your System folder that may not work with System 7 (see Figure 2-3). Clicking on **Move Items** moves the offending programs out of your System folder to a folder called May Not Work with System 7. It's a good idea to move them out for now. To move these programs:

9

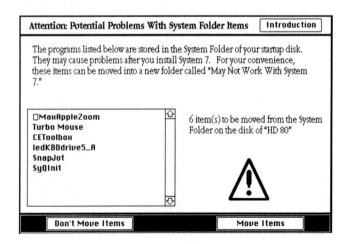

Figure 2-3. Possible problems in the System folder with the Compatibility Checker.

1. Click on **Move Items** and then click on the **OK** button to confirm the move.

2. When the Checker is done, printing the list of incompatible files for later review is a good idea. Click on **Report** to print the Compatibility Report.

3. Select **Quit** at the bottom of the screen to exit the Compatibility Checker.

   Lesson 4, "What To Do with Your Old Files," contains information on what to do with these files from your Compatibility Report. After you've finished the installation, be sure to go over that lesson.

   In this lesson you've learned how to prepare for installing System 7. The next lesson will teach you how to install your new system so that you can put it to use quickly.

Lesson 3
Installing System 7

In this lesson you'll learn how to install System 7.

After you have prepared yourself for installing System 7 by backing up and removing incompatible files from your hard drive, you can proceed to the actual installation process.

Installing

Installing System 7 requires the use of the Apple Installer on Install Disk 1. There are two ways you can install System 7. You can install System 7 over a previous version of the system software, or you can install on a system less hard drive. The advantage of installing over your previous version is that the Installer automatically updates all of your old fonts, Desk Accessories, startup documents, and other add-ons, and saves space by erasing your old 6.0.x files. Installing on an empty second hard drive has the advantage of allowing you to switch between your System 6 on the old hard drive and System 7 on your fresh hard drive if any important applications aren't compatible or if something goes wrong.

You also have two other choices—whether to install using the *easy* method or to install using the *customize* method. The easy install method is quicker and requires less

11

work, but the customized installation method saves space on your hard drive. Unless you have limited hard drive space (as many Macintosh users do), using the easy installation is a good idea.

Installing—the Easy Method

To install System 7, follow these steps:

1. Restart your computer with Install Disk 1. Your computer will start up right into the Installer. Click O K on the opening screen.

2. A window like the one shown in Figure 3-1 will open. Click on Switch Disk until the screen displays the name of the hard drive you want to install on. Now's your chance to choose which way you want to install— on a fresh hard drive or over your current system.

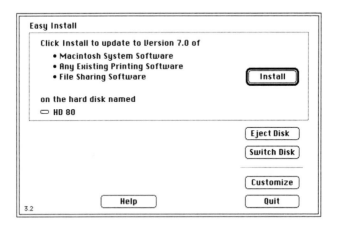

Figure 3-1. The Easy Install of System 7.

3. Click Install.

4. The Installer will take several moments finding which disks it needs in the installation. During this time, make sure you have the full set of System 7 upgrade disks (see Table 3-1). You should have eight floppy disks if you are using 800K disks, and you should have six floppies if using 1.44M disks.

5. Insert the disks as prompted by the Installer. This process may take several minutes.

6. When the Installer is done, it will present a dialog box asking what you want to do. Click **Restart** and your Macintosh will restart running System 7.

Table 3-1. System 7 upgrade disk sets.

800K disk set	1.44M disk set
Install 1	Install 1
Install 2	Install 2
Install 3	Fonts
Fonts	Disk Tools
Disk Tools	Printing
Printing	Tidbits
Tidbits	
More Tidbits	

Customized Installation of System 7

If space on your hard drive is extremely limited, you can use the customize method to install a smaller version of the System files. To install using this method, follow these steps:

1. Click `Customize` from the Installer window. The screen will change to look like Figure 3-2.

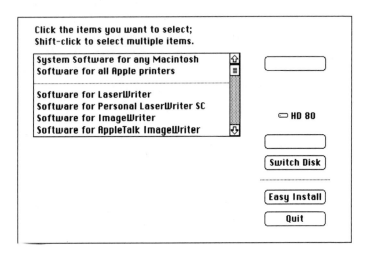

Figure 3-2. Customized Install window.

2. If you have an Apple printer, scroll down the list until you see your printer listed.

   Non-Apple printers If you have a non-Apple printer, it's a good idea to contact your printer's manufacturer and make sure that the printer is compatible with System 7. If it's not, you can get out of the installation at this point by clicking on `Quit`.

3. Press the Shift key and simultaneously click on the name of your printer. If you're going to be using more than one printer, hold down the Shift key and click on the names of any additional printers you may use.

4. If you are on a network, scroll down and Shift-click on `File Sharing Software`.

5. Scroll until you see your computer listed in the System Software for... section.

6. Shift-click on the name of your computer. If, for example, you have a Macintosh IIsi, Shift-click on System Software for Macintosh IIsi.

7. If you have more than one hard drive, click on Switch Disk until the name of your hard drive shows up.

8. Click on Install.

9. The Installer assesses which disks you need to install. When the Installer prompts you for a specific disk, be sure to insert it.

10. When the installation is complete, a window opens asking if you want to quit or restart. Click on Restart and your Macintosh will start with System 7.

In this lesson you've learned how to do the easy and customized installations of System 7. In the next lesson you'll learn what to do with the list you generated from the Compatibility Checker and all of your old System files.

Lesson 4

What To Do with Your Old Files

In this lesson you'll learn how to deal with applications and files created with System 6.

The Compatibility Checker List

In Lesson 2 you made a list of all the applications on your hard drive with the Compatibility Checker stack. The list starts by giving some general descriptions about upgrading to System 7. If you have the time, read through the information; if not, you can skip ahead. There may be some CAUTION remarks before the actual list of items checked. Most likely, they will tell you that you either have incompatible programs in your System folder or that you have some sort of security or virus protection software enabled. Be sure to heed Apple's advice in these areas.

The Compatibility Report itemizes the applications on the hard drive the Compatibility Checker scanned. Columns show the item checked, your version, the status of the program, and notes. Take a look at each of these items in some more detail.

- *Item checked*—Lists the name of the file checked.

- *Your version*—Tells the version of the item that you have present on your hard drive.

- *Status*—Tells how compatible your item is with System 7. Your status message is Compatible, Mostly Compatible, Must Upgrade, or Not Available. You'll learn more about status in the next section.

- *Notes*—Contains information needed for upgrading items. This column tells the version number (if available) that fixes the incompatibilities with System 7 and, in some cases, what the item is specifically incompatible with. If an item isn't compatible with a certain feature of System 7, you can turn that feature off.

Status

If a program is Compatible with System 7, then there's no need to worry about it. It will probably work perfectly with the new system.

Mostly Compatible programs work most of the time. If a mostly compatible item is listed with a phone number at the end of the compatibility list, then you should call the software publishers and ask for an upgrade. You can obtain upgrades normally for only a fraction of the original program's price and, in some cases, upgrades are even free.

Must Upgrade programs will not work with System 7. Call the developer to see if they have an upgrade available. Some retailers may have upgrades but usually charge the full price. Developers often offer discounts to registered users.

The Notes Column

Looking through your Compatibility Report, you will see two kinds of items in the notes column. On the left side, there are numbers. These are the version numbers of the files that are compatible with System 7. If an upgrade version is present, then be sure to mention it when you call the developer of the program. Also, there may be two note letters in some columns. Following is a list of some of the notes:

AD—The program is not compatible with 32-bit addressing. If you have a Macintosh LC, IIsi, IIci, or IIfx, take the following steps to turn off 32-bit addressing before running this program. If you don't have one of these models, disregard this incompatibility.

1. Select Control Panels from the Apple menu.

2. Double-click on the Memory control panel (see Figure 4-1).

Memory

Figure 4-1. The Memory control panel.

3. If the 32-bit Addressing box is checked, uncheck it.

CD—Contact the developer for more information about compatible versions.

FR—A free upgrade is available. Call the developer.

FS—File sharing does not work with this program. To turn file sharing off, follow these steps:

1. Select Control Panel from the Apple menu.

2. Double-click on Sharing Setup.

3. The window will open, as in Figure 4-2. If the Status window for file sharing (the one in the middle) says that file sharing is on, click the Stop button under the folder icon for File Sharing.

```
▤□▤▤▤▤▤▤▤▤▤▤▤ Sharing Setup ▤▤▤▤▤▤▤▤▤▤▤▤▤
┌─┐
│ │   Network Identity
└─┘
        Owner Name:     ███████████████████████
        Owner Passw...  [ ●●●●●           ]
        Macintosh Na... [ Joe                 ]
   ┌─┐
   │ │  File Sharing
   └─┘        ..Status.........................................
        ┌──────────┐  File sharing is off. Click Start to allow other
        │  Start   │  users to access shared folders.
        └──────────┘
   ◇    Program Linking
   ◇◇         ..Status.........................................
        ┌──────────┐  Program linking is off. Click Start to allow
        │  Start   │  other users to link to your shared programs.
        └──────────┘
```

Figure 4-2. The Sharing Setup control panel.

MO—These items have been moved out of your System folder into the May Not Work with System 7 folder by the Compatibility Checker.

RI —This item is replaced by an item on one of your System 7 disks.

TT —Large TrueType fonts are not supported. If a program has this message in the notes column, you probably do not need to upgrade.

UN —These items are unnecessary with System 7. Most items marked with UN are utilities that gave your System 6 Macintosh one of the new features of System 7.

UP —Upgrades are available from dealers, BBSs, and users' groups.

UR —This item should be upgraded although it may work.

UM —This item will not work with Virtual Memory. To turn Virtual Memory off, follow these steps (see Lesson 15 to learn more about Virtual Memory):

1. Select Control Panel from the Apple menu.

2. Double-click on the Memory control panel.

3. If Virtual Memory is switched on when the control panel opens, click the Off button (see Figure 4-3).

4. Click on the Close box to close the Memory control panel.

Desk Accessories (DAs)

System 7 automatically takes your Desk Accessories and puts them in the Apple Menu Items folder. (For more information on this folder, see Lesson 8). The Compatibility Checker, however, does not check your DAs to see if they are compatible.

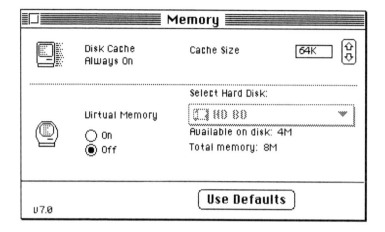

Figure 4-3. The Memory control panel.

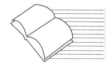

DAs Desk Accessories are small applications that are launched from the Apple menu in System 6. System 7 automatically puts DAs in the Apple menu, and like other applications, you can use DAs anywhere in System 7.

Because Apple doesn't check your Desk Accessories, you'll have to check them manually. In the Finder, select each Desk Accessory from the Apple menu. Check each of the features to make sure that it's working fine. If it doesn't work normally or *crashes* the computer, then follow these steps to remove a bad Desk Accessory:

1. Double-click on your hard disk icon to open it into its window.

2. Double-click on the System folder to open it.

21

3. Find the Apple Menu Items folder and double-click on it to open it (see Figure 4-4).

Apple Menu Items

Figure 4-4. The Apple Menu Items folder.

4. Click on the Desk Accessory you want to remove.

5. Drag the Desk Accessory into the Trash and select Empty Trash from the Special menu.

When you're checking Desk Accessories... It's possible that some DAs will make the computer freeze (not allow any actions), create a system error, or make a spectacular crash (with full static light show on your monitor). These failures occur with incompatible software. Simply use the restart switch on your computer, or turn it off and on again if you don't have a reset switch installed.

In this lesson you've learned what to do with your old files and Desk Accessories. In the next lesson you will learn about some of the refinements of System 7.

Lesson 5
System 7
Refinements

In this lesson you'll learn some of the changes to the Finder in System 7.

System 7 incorporates many new features in the Finder, making the Finder easier to learn and making you more productive.

The Finder The Finder is the technical name for the Macintosh desktop. Refer to the "System Software Primer" at the end of the book if you are unclear on this terminology.

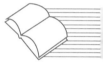

Outline Views

In the Finder there are various ways to view files, which you can choose under the View menu. Icon and Small Icon views display files by showing icons in their windows as the old Finder did, but all of the other View commands incorporate a new system called *outline viewing*. Now, when you view by Name, Size, Kind, Label, Version, or Comment, you'll notice arrows next to your folders.

When you click on one of the arrows, it turns downward and displays the contents of that folder indented under it. In Figure 5-1, the 10 Min Guide Sys. 7 folder is expanded.

Looking at the window's contents in outline view makes navigating and looking in folders quicker and easier. Previously, you had to double-click on the folder to open it and then open another folder within it until you found the application or document you wanted. Now, by expanding outlines by clicking on the arrows, you can quickly and easily see the contents of your folders.

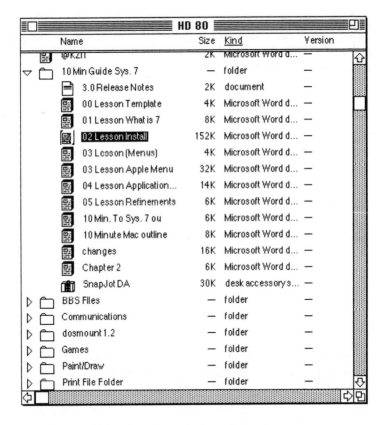

Figure 5-1. An expanded outline view.

Shrinking your outline To shrink the outline to its original state, click on the downward pointing arrows to close up the expanded portion of the outline.

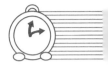

Renaming Files

System 7 has slightly changed the method for renaming files. To rename a file, disk, or folder, follow these steps:

1. If it is not already selected, click once on the name of the icon to select it.

2. Move the mouse pointer to the name of the icon and click again. A rectangular box will appear around the name (see Figure 5-2).

Figure 5-2. The Syquest F disk with the icon unselected, icon selected, and with the name selected.

3. Make sure that a box appears around the name. If it does not, click the mouse somewhere else on the blank desktop and then repeat the process. Then the name of the file is selected.

Desktop The desktop is the basic workspace in the background on your Macintosh.

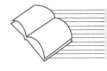

4. To rename the file, simply type the new name and it will replace the selected name. When you select the name in this manner, you also can cut, copy, and paste as if you were working in a word processor.

Finding Files

Before System 7, you needed either the File Find DA or a third party utility to find files on your hard disk drives. Now Apple has incorporated basic file finding into System 7. This new feature will search through your hard disks to find files with certain characteristics.

To find a file by name:

1. Select Find... from the File menu.

2. When the dialog box appears, type the name or portion of the name you want to find (see Figure 5-3).

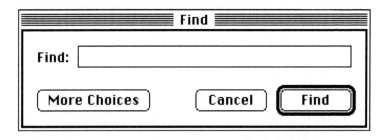

Figure 5-3. The Find... dialog box.

3. Click the Find button. The Finder will look through each disk on the desktop and open a window where the first occurrence of the file name appears. Select Find Again from the File menu to search for the next occurrence of that name in a file name.

By selecting More Choices, you will see another dialog box with more advanced finding features, which allow you to search on any disk on your computer by size, kind, label, date created, date modified, or comments (see Figure 5-4).

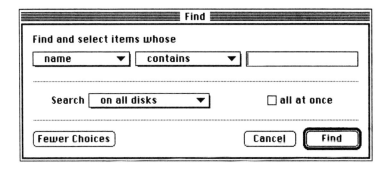

Figure 5-4. Advanced finding features.

Balloon Help

System 7 also provides a better system for getting help with the Finder and many applications. When you turn on Balloon Help, a description is given for every notable item that you point to with the mouse pointer on-screen (see Figure 5-5).

At this point, the Finder, most Apple software products, and some other applications support Balloon Help. Most new applications being developed will support it, and many updates of current applications will include Balloon Help.

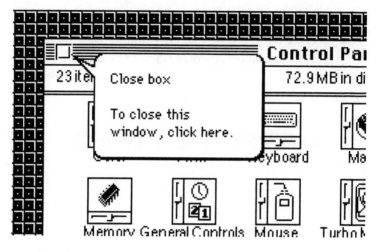

Figure 5-5. A balloon giving information on the close box in the Finder.

To turn Balloon Help on:

1. Click on the icon resembling a balloon containing a question mark, located on the right of the Applications menu. The Balloon Help menu will open up.

   The Applications menu You use the Applications menu to select which program you want to use. In this case, the menu is probably represented by a small Macintosh icon if the Finder is open. For more information on how to use the Applications menu, see Lesson 10.

2. Select Show Balloons from the Balloon Help menu.

   Balloon Help may be annoying if you have already learned the basics of a program. To turn Balloon Help off, select Hide Balloons from the Balloon Help menu.

This lesson has shown you how to use some of the new features of the Finder. The next lesson will show you the arrangement of the System folder and how to add fonts and sounds.

The New System Folder

In this lesson you'll learn about the new arrangement of the System folder.

That Was Then ...

In older versions of the Macintosh system, Desk Accessories, INITs (small utilities that load at startup), control panels, PostScript fonts, preference files, and a few other files either would be dumped into the System folder or installed in the System file with the Font/DA Mover. Using this method often resulted in huge and unmanageable System folders. System 7 changes this operation by creating a new group of folders for different items within the System folder and changes the format of the system itself (see Figure 6-1). Now, take a closer look at each of the new folders.

The Apple Menu Items Folder

The Apple Menu Items folder holds items that you can use through the Apple menu. You can launch or open files placed in this folder by selecting them from the Apple menu. Refer to Lesson 8 for more detailed information on how to add Desk Accessories, applications, and other files.

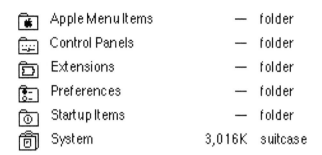

Figure 6-1. The new folders and System file.

The Extensions Folder

The Extensions folder holds the following files that make your Mac more useful:

INITs—INITs (startup documents) from System 6 are now called *Extensions* in System 7. If an item is both a control panel AND an INIT, then it should go in the Control Panels folder instead.

Printer Drivers—These documents are used by the Chooser DA to tell your Mac how to communicate with the printers you have installed.

Extensions—These new System 7 files from Apple and third party vendors enhance the use of your Macintosh.

PostScript Fonts—If you have a PostScript printer (for example, the LaserWriter), then any additional fonts will probably go in the Extensions folder.

31

If your older system files don't work... Some older system files made for System 6.0.x may be put in the Extensions folder by the Finder. If the files don't work, try taking them out of the Extensions folder and putting them in the System folder.

Startup Items Folder

In System 6.0.x, you selected items for startup from a Set Startup selection in the Special menu in the Finder. System 7 changes this procedure. If you want a program to run on startup or a certain document to open when you start your Macintosh, you can put these files in the Startup Items folder. If you don't want to dump your files in the Startup Items folder because they would disorganize your hard disk drive, making aliases of your files or applications and placing them in the Startup Items folder instead might be a good idea. (Lesson 14 contains more information on aliases.)

Control Panels Folder

The Control Panels folder holds all of the control panels (see Figure 6-2). Control panels are files that enable you to adjust and fine-tune your Macintosh, such as changing the speaker volume or the desktop pattern. Some commercial programs also use a control panel to control their utility software.

You can access the Control Panels folder either by opening it manually or by selecting it in the Apple menu. And you can access individual control panels by double-clicking on their icons in the Control Panels folder.

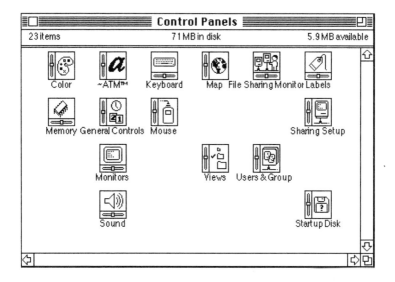

Figure 6-2. The Control Panels folder.

Preferences Folder

Various applications use the Preferences folder to store their Preferences files. Preferences files contain information that allows the application to retain the settings or alterations you have made.

System File

The System file of System 7 is different from the System file in System 6 in that:

- The 6.0.x System file needed utilities like the Font/DA Mover to add features to it. You can now add fonts and sounds to the System file by dragging them into the System file window.

33

- The 6.0.x System file contained fonts, Desk Accessories, and sounds. The System 7 System file now contains only fonts and sounds; Desk Accessories are in the Apple Menu Items folder.

Adding Fonts and Sounds

To add fonts and sounds to the new System file:

1. Quit all applications.

2. In the Finder, open both the System folder and the folder that contains the font or sound suitcase so that both are visible at the same time.

 Suitcase A suitcase is a file that holds fonts, sounds, and Desk Accessories. System 7 treats suitcases as folders; you can open them by double-clicking on them.

3. Double-click on the font or sound suitcase to open it.

4. Select the fonts or sounds you want to copy, or choose **Select All** from the File menu in the Finder.

5. Click on one of the selected items and drag it to the System file icon. Then, wait as the files copy.

 Confused programs It's a good idea to restart your computer after installing fonts or sounds. Utilities residing in your computer's memory might get confused by the new fonts or sounds.

This lesson has given you an overview of the new arrangement of the System folder and how to install fonts and sounds. The next lesson will describe the new Control Panels folder in detail.

Lesson 7
The Control Panels Folder

In this lesson you'll learn about the new Control Panels folder.

The New Control Panel Format

As mentioned in the preceding lesson, the format for the control panels changed from System 6 to System 7. In System 6 the control panel was a Desk Accessory. You could add additional panels by dragging them into the System folder. This arrangement caused cluttered System folders and was hard to use because the scrolling control panel selector often moved too quickly, making it difficult to stop on a particular panel. Also, you could not see all of your control panels at once (see Figure 7-1). System 7 makes the Control Panel a folder in your System folder (see Figure 7-2). This new system makes your System folder neater and makes choosing and viewing your control panels much easier.

Opening the Control Panels

You can open the control panels one of two ways. To open the control panels from either the Finder or any application, select **Control Panels** from the Apple menu. This takes you back to the Finder if you are working in another application and opens the control panels for you.

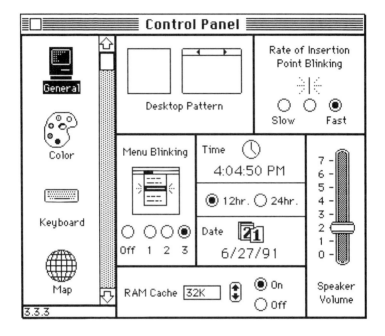

Figure 7-1. The old Control Panel.

You also can open the control panels directly from the System folder. To do this:

1. Open your hard disk drive by double-clicking on its icon.

2. Open your System folder.

3. Open the Control Panels folder from within the System folder. Sometimes you must use the scroll bars on the right side and bottom of the window to find your Control Panels folder. Then the Control Panels window will open for you.

37

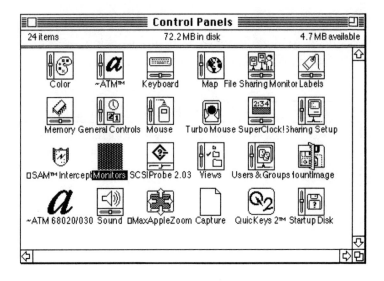

Figure 7-2. The new Control Panel.

How To View Your Control Panels

One of the features of the new Control Panels folder is that you can organize your control panels in many different ways using the View menu of the Finder. Icon view is the system's default for viewing your control panels. In Icon view you can arrange the icons of the control panels however you want. You can also view the control panels by Small Icon, which shrinks the sizes of the icons so that you can fit more in the window. And you can also display your control panels in list form, organized by Name, Date, Size, Version, or Label (see Figures 7-3 and 7-4).

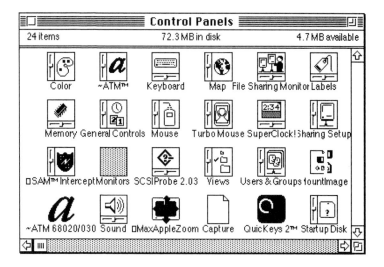

Figure 7-3. Control panels viewed by Icon.

1. Select **Control Panels** from the Apple menu.

2. Select the way you want to view the control panels from the View menu.

3. The Control Panels view method will change according to your selection. Keep trying different views until you find one that fits your preferences.

If you can't see some control panels... You may want to resize the window using the resize box in the lower right corner of the window so that you can see all of the control panels.

Name	Size	Kind	Label	Version
▣MaxAppleZoom	16K	control panel	—	1.1
▣SAM™ Intercept	182K	control panel	—	3.0.0
Capture	54K	control panel	—	4.0a18
Color	12K	control panel	—	7.0
File Sharing Monitor	4K	control panel	—	7.0b6
General Controls	16K	control panel	—	7.0
Keyboard	8K	control panel	—	7.0
Labels	4K	control panel	—	7.0
Map	28K	control panel	—	7.0
Memory	28K	control panel	—	7.0
Monitors	40K	control panel	—	—
MountImage	12K	control panel	—	1.2ß1
Mouse	8K	control panel	—	7.0
QuicKeys 2™	244K	control panel	—	2.1ß9
SCSIProbe 2.03	6K	control panel	—	2.03
Sharing Setup	4K	control panel	—	7.0
Sound	18K	control panel	—	7.0
Startup Disk	6K	control panel	—	7.0
SuperClock!	18K	control panel	—	3.9
Turbo Mouse	14K	control panel	—	1.2
Users & Groups	4K	control panel	—	7.0
Views	4K	control panel	—	7.0

Figure 7-4. Control panels viewed by Name.

Control Panels Outside of the Folder

In System 7, it's also possible to have control panels outside of the Control Panels folder. If, for example, you use the Monitors control panel often, you might want to put it on your desktop. If so, just select that control panel and drag it out of the Control Panels folder. Also, you might want to make an alias of the control panel to use it in other places.

Overview of Control Panels

System 7 comes with a basic set of control panels. Following are some of them. (Networking control panels will be covered in Lesson 16.)

Color—Allows you to set the color of selected text if you have color capability.

File Sharing Monitor—Monitors file sharing on your Macintosh (see Lesson 16).

General Controls—Changes basic information like the time, background, how fast your cursor blinks, etc. (see Figure 7-5).

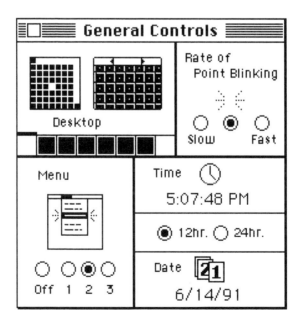

Figure 7-5. The General Controls control panel.

Keyboard—Enables you to fine-tune your keyboard.

Labels—Sets information on the labeling feature of System 7 (see Lesson 9).

Map—Displays a world map and lets you see what time it is in other parts of the world (see Figure 7-6).

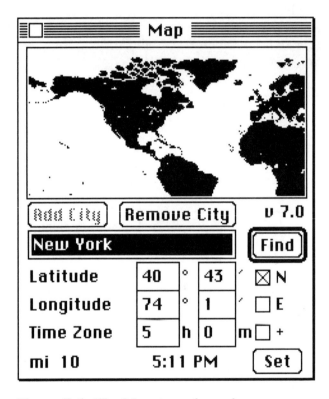

Figure 7-6. The Map control panel.

Memory—Enables you to change information on how your Macintosh deals with memory (see Lesson 15).

Monitors—Enables you to set color/grayscale levels on monitors or color machines and set information if you have more than one monitor.

Mouse—Changes mouse settings.

Sharing Setup—Sets up file sharing on your Macintosh (see Lesson 16).

Sound—Chooses what sound you want as your beep sound and sets the volume on your Macintosh (see Figure 7-7).

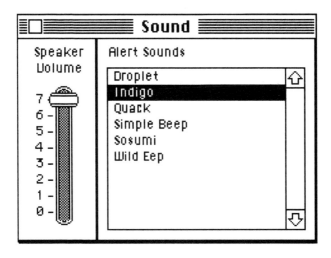

Figure 7-7. The Sound control panel.

Users & Groups—Defines who can use what parts of your Macintosh if file sharing is turned on (see Lesson 17).

Views—Changes the way the Finder displays information.

In this lesson you have learned about the new control panels and how to view them. In the next lesson you will learn about the new Apple menu.

Lesson 8
The New
Apple Menu

In this lesson you'll learn to use the new Apple menu.

What's Different?

The Apple menu in the old system was simply a place to get information about the program you were using or to access a Desk Accessory. The most common DAs are the Alarm Clock, Key Caps, Chooser, and Control Panel. You could install these and other DAs into the System file with a program called the Font/DA Mover. In System 7 Apple has renovated the Apple menu and added several new features as well.

The new Apple menu is a folder called the Apple Menu Items folder inside the System folder (see Figure 8-1).

Apple Menu Items

Figure 8-1. Apple Menu Items folder (within the System folder).

Now DAs are individual applications inside the Apple Menu Items folder. But the most important new feature is

44

that you can put almost anything inside the Apple Menu Items folder and launch it from the Apple menu. Putting an application or a document inside this folder enables you to launch the program or file by just pulling down the menu and selecting it.

This folder system makes the Font/DA Mover obsolete and provides a new way to install DAs and other items. Fonts are also affected by this change and are installed without the Font/DA Mover. Refer to Lesson 6 for more information on installing fonts.

Aliases An alias is a small file that you can set to act like a file on your disk. For example, opening an alias of your word processing document opens the actual document, even if the document and alias are in two separate folders. More information on aliases is available in Lesson 14.

How To Install DAs

If you update your old system using the Installer, System 7 will automatically convert any old DAs for you and add in new versions of the standard Apple DAs such as the Alarm Clock, Battery, Chooser, Key Caps, Notepad, Scrapbook, and a new version of the game. If you buy any new DAs or want to install old ones not updated during the installation, follow this procedure:

1. In the Finder, open both the System folder and the disk/ folder where the DA suitcase is located. Figure 8-2 shows typical DA icons.

45

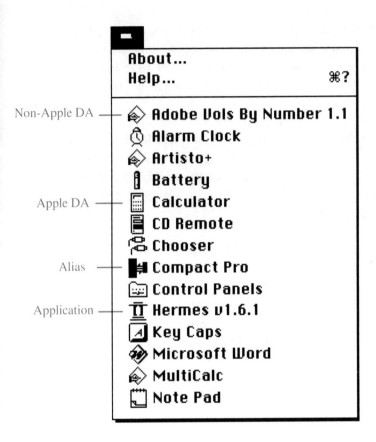

Figure 8-2. Typical DA icons.

2. Double-click on the DA suitcase (see Figure 8-3). The suitcase will open and show a window similar to Figure 8-4.

Figure 8-3. A DA suitcase.

How to distinguish a suitcase window You can distinguish a suitcase window from other windows by the small suitcase icon, which is located below the close box in the upper left corner of the window.

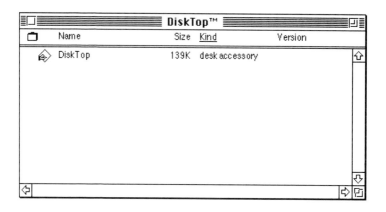

Figure 8-4. A typical DA window showing the Disktop Desk Accessory.

3. Click on the DA you want to install and, holding down the mouse button, drag the DA to the Apple Menu Items folder.

The next time you open your Apple menu, the DA you just installed will be listed.

To remove a Desk Accessory... If you accidentally installed a Desk Accessory you didn't want, you still can remove it. To remove a file from the Apple Menu Items folder, just open the folder, select the item you want to remove, drag it to the Trash, and select **Empty Trash** from the Special menu.

Other Items for the Apple Menu Items Folder

DAs are not the only files that you can place in the new Apple Menu Items folder; now you can include applications, documents, and aliases. To add an application file to the Apple menu, follow these steps:

1. Open the System folder.

2. Drag the application icon to the Apple Menu Items folder.

Now the installed file will appear in the Apple menu. Selecting the file will launch it as if you had double-clicked it in the Finder.

This lesson has shown you what the new Apple menu is and how to install DAs, applications, and documents into it. In the next lesson you'll learn how to set up and view labels.

Using the Label Menu

In this lesson you'll learn the various ways to use the Label menu.

System 6 contained a menu in the Finder that enabled you to color the icons of files, applications, and folders on color Macintosh systems, thus allowing you to identify them quickly and sort by color. System 7 expands this feature to the new labeling system, which allows you to assign various items in your system to different labels and then find and sort by these labels for increased productivity. For example, you might want to tag all files of a certain project with a certain label. Then you can sort by label to distinguish these files from others in an overcrowded folder.

Setting Up Labels

Before you can use labels effectively, you should customize the names. (Apple default names are nondescriptive; for example, Hot, Cool, Personal, Project 1, and Project 2.) Many people choose names to specify projects or file types (that is, newsletter, games, etc.).

1. Select Control Panels from the Apple menu. The Control Panels window will appear, showing the various control panel devices installed on your system.

2. Scroll until you find the Labels icon (see Figure 9-1).

Figure 9-1. The Labels control panel icon.

3. Double-click on the icon. Then the Labels control panel will open, presenting a column of labels on the right and colors on the left (see Figure 9-2). If you have a color monitor, the colors match the color names in the figure.

Figure 9-2. The open Labels control panel.

4. To change the label name, click on the name of the label you want and type the new name.

Black-and-white labels If you have a black-and-white monitor, it's a good idea to make sure all of your label colors are black because programs or documents labeled white often have unintelligible icons.

Changing the colors accompanying your new labels is often useful. Double-clicking on one of the colors will bring up the standard Apple Color Picker (see Figure 9-3). Click anywhere in the color wheel to choose the hue and then adjust the brightness using the scroll bar at the right. Clicking o k will set the current label to the color selected.

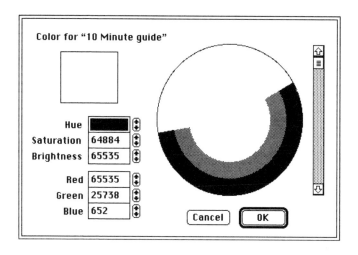

Figure 9-3. The standard Apple Color Picker.

Viewing by Label

The label feature of System 7 is most useful in the Finder, where you can sort windows by label. If, for instance, you have labels for different projects you are working on or have a different label for different types of files (that is, applications, utilities, desktop publishing, etc.), viewing by label allows the Finder to sort these files automatically by their categories. To view by label in the Finder:

1. Click on the title bar of the window you want to view by label to make the window active.

2. When the window becomes active, select **by Label** from the View menu.

Now your selected window is sorted by label, as in Figure 9-4.

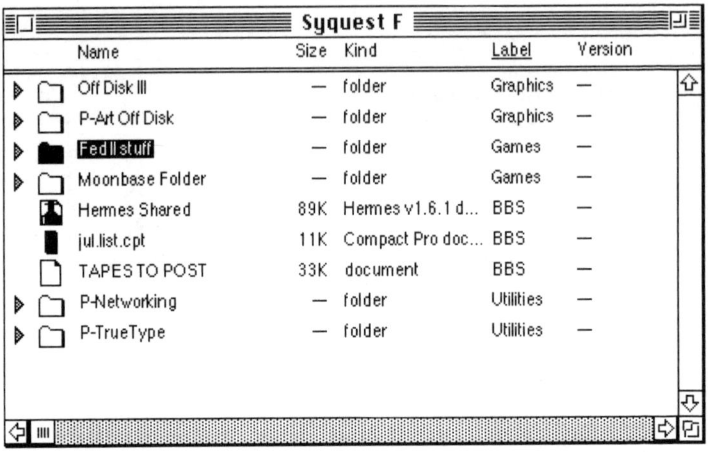

	Name	Size	Kind	<u>Label</u>	Version
▷ ◻	Off Disk III	—	folder	Graphics	—
▷ ◻	P-Art Off Disk	—	folder	Graphics	—
▷ ◼	Fed II stuff	—	folder	Games	—
▷ ◻	Moonbase Folder	—	folder	Games	—
	Hermes Shared	89K	Hermes v1.6.1 d...	BBS	—
	jul.list.cpt	11K	Compact Pro doc...	BBS	—
	TAPES TO POST	33K	document	BBS	—
▷ ◻	P-Networking	—	folder	Utilities	—
▷ ◻	P-TrueType	—	folder	Utilities	—

(Window title: Syquest F)

Figure 9-4. A window sorted by label.

Finding by Labels

You also can use labels in the finding process. In Lesson 5 you learned briefly about the advanced finding features of the Find command. To access the Find command:

1. Select **Find** from the File menu in the Finder.

2. When the Find window opens, click on **More Choices**.

3. A larger Find window will open (see Figure 9-5). Pull down the Name menu on the left side of the window.

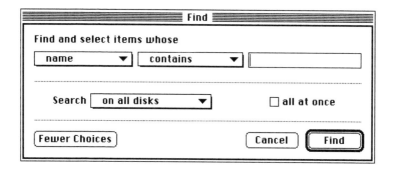

Figure 9-5. The larger Find window.

4. When the menu appears on the right, pull it down and select the label you want to find.

5. Click the **Find** button to locate the first file of the label selected. To find the next, select **Find Again** from the File menu in the Finder.

> **To find quickly...** The shortcut to open the Find window is Command-F. The shortcut to Find Again is Command-G.

This lesson has taught you about the use of labels in System 7. In the next lesson you'll learn more about the Applications menu.

The Applications Menu

In this lesson you'll learn how to use the new Applications menu.

Understanding Macintosh Multitasking

The Applications menu is a new menu present at all times in the upper right corner of the screen. This new interface for *multitasking* is simpler to use and more refined (see Figure 10-1).

Multitasking Multitasking enables your Macintosh to run more than one application at one time. For example, with multitasking you can keep your word processor, paint program, and database program open at the same time and switch between them without having to exit any of them. Multitasking also allows you to keep the Finder open at all times so that you can copy and manipulate files. It also allows background printing.

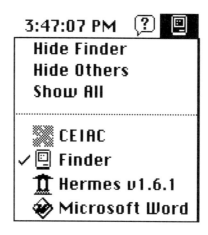

Figure 10-1. The Applications menu.

In the old Macintosh System, you could switch on a program named MultiFinder, which allowed multitasking. MultiFinder, however, wasn't a very good way to multitask. You had to turn it on and off from the Finder, many applications did not support it, background copying and formatting was not allowed, and the interface was clumsy. (You had to click in the upper right corner of the screen or select from the Apple menu to change applications.)

Switching Between Applications

When you are in the Finder and you open an application, the application becomes active and its menu bar is visible at the top of the screen. Other programs may be in memory at the same time, but they are deactivated in the background.

Active An *active* application is currently in use. A *deactivated* application is still running and can be seen in the background, but you must select and activate it before use.

To deactivate the application you are currently working with and select another, you may click in any visible portion of the program you want to choose. But in many cases, the window of the active program hides all other activities. To use the Applications menu to switch:

1. Click on the Applications menu icon (the picture of your current application to the right of the balloon).

2. Hold down the mouse button and select the application you want to switch to. Figure 10-2 shows several application windows open on the desktop.

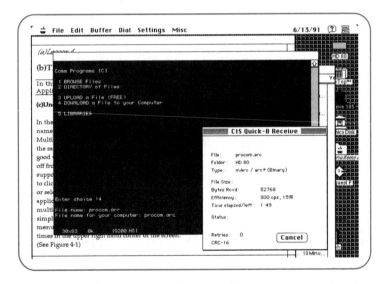

Figure 10-2. Multiple application windows open at one time.

When you are multitasking, it's easy to get lost and not know what application you're in. Following are some ways you can tell where you are:

- The icon of the application you are using is shown in the upper right corner of the screen. If it's a Macintosh icon, then you're probably in the Finder.

- The menu bar is appropriate for the application you're using. Menu bars change when you switch applications.

- The program you are using is checked when you pull down the Applications menu.

- The About... selection in the Apple menu tells you what application you're in (that is, if you are in TeachText, it would say **About TeachText**).

Using the Hide All and Show All Commands

When you switched between applications, you probably noticed the two Hide commands and the Show All command listed in the Applications menu. They are useful when your desktop becomes cluttered with bits and pieces of applications and the Finder is showing behind your active program.

To hide just your current application and return to the Finder, select the **Hide [current application]** selection. Figures 10-3 and 10-4 show the desktop before and after hiding applications. Although your application seems to disappear, you can retrieve it by selecting it in the Applications menu (as detailed in the preceding section).

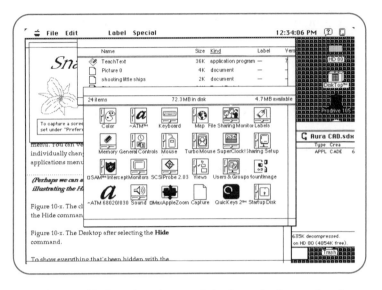

Figure 10-3. The cluttered desktop before selecting the Hide command.

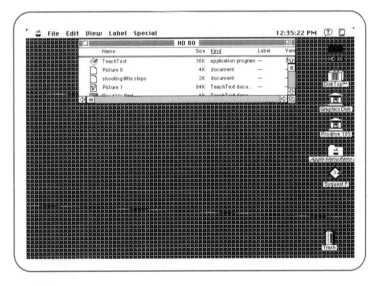

Figure 10-4. The desktop after selecting the Hide command.

To hide everything that you're not currently working on, select **Hide All** from the Applications menu. You can view everything again by changing to each application individually using the Applications menu.

To show everything that you have hidden with the two Hide commands, select **Show All** from the Applications menu. All applications will be shown in the background.

In this lesson you've learned how to use the Applications menu and the new multitasking features of System 7. In the next lesson you will learn how to navigate the system with the keyboard and pop-up menus.

Navigating

In this lesson you'll learn how to use the new navigation features of the Finder.

What's New?

The System 7 Finder has several new navigation features. Pop-up menus allow you to open folders quickly, and the new keyboard shortcuts enable you to navigate through the Finder more quickly.

Pop-up Menus

When you open folders in the Finder, you (like most people) probably close other folders to clear your desktop. This results in folders nested deep in your hard disk with no easy way to open the original folders that contain them. In Figure 11-1, for example, if you close folders A and B and leave folder C open, there is no easy way under System 6 to open folder B again without opening the hard disk and folder A first.

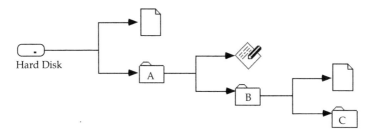

Figure 11-1. A sample folder structure.

Pop-up menus in System 7 allow you to open folders easily. To use pop-up menus, follow these steps:

1. Select the window of the folder that is contained in the folder you want to open.

2. Hold down the Command key (⌘) and click on the folder name in the title bar of the window. A menu will pop up showing all of the current folder's parent folders (see Figure 11-2).

Figure 11-2. A pop-up menu.

3. Choose which folder you want to open from the list by clicking on it. Then the specified folder will open.

Keyboard Shortcuts

One of the new features of the System 7 Finder is a new set of keyboard shortcuts. In the past you could use the keyboard in the Finder only for the various command keys, which are marked by the clover signs and letters in the menus (see Figure 11-3).

```
┌─────────────────────────────┐
│ File                        │
├─────────────────────────────┤
│  New Folder        ⌘N       │
│  Open              ⌘O       │
│  Print             ⌘P       │
│  Close Window      ⌘W       │
│ ............................│
│  Get Info          ⌘I       │
│  Sharing...                 │
│  Duplicate         ⌘D       │
│  Make Alias                 │
│  Put Away          ⌘Y       │
│ ............................│
│  Find...           ⌘F       │
│  Find Again        ⌘G       │
│ ............................│
│  Page Setup...              │
│  Print Window...            │
└─────────────────────────────┘
```

Figure 11-3. A menu with command key equivalents.

Now, the Finder has a full set of keyboard commands, which make the Finder more efficient than the standard mouse movements. Lists of these key equivalents can be displayed in the Finder in a series of windows on-screen. To access the cards (windows), follow these steps:

1. Choose **Finder Shortcuts** from the Balloon Help menu.

2. Click the **Next** and **Previous** buttons to scroll through the five cards (see Figure 11-4).

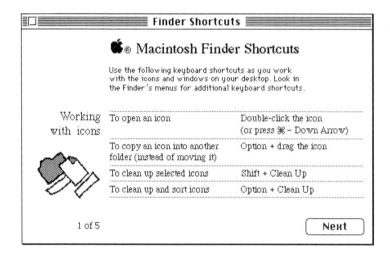

Figure 11-4. The first card in the Finder Shortcuts.

Following is a list of some of the other useful Finder Shortcuts:

- To select an icon from an active window, begin typing its name.

- To select the next icon alphabetically, hit the Tab key.

- To select the preceding icon alphabetically, hold down the Shift key and press the Tab key.

- To select icons while in Icon view, use the arrow keys. For example, hitting the left-arrow key selects the icon to the left of your current position.

- To close all windows, hold down the Option key and click the `Close` button on any window.

- To change the way you view icons in an Outline view, click on a view title (that is, Name, Size, Kind, Label) in the window header.

- To collapse and expand the outline of a selected folder, hold down the Command key ($\mathcal{H}$) and use the left and right arrows.

Other New Navigating Features

In addition to pop-up menus and keyboard equivalents, the System 7 Finder also incorporates the following new features:

- *Scrolling while dragging*—If there are more items in a folder than can be displayed in a Finder window, the scroll bars become active so that you can scroll to see all items. In the System 6 Finder, there was no easy way to select items not visible in the window. System 7 automatically scrolls when you are selecting more than one item so that you can include icons not currently in view.

- *New Trash*—In the System 6 Finder, the Trash was automatically emptied whenever you restarted or shut down your computer, or whenever you loaded an application. This was an inconvenience because many times you probably "threw away" important information by mistake. Now, when you drag items to the Trash to throw them out, they stay in the Trash until you select Empty Trash from the Special menu. You can double-click on the Trash as if it were a folder and then drag items back to your hard disk to recover trashed files.

In this lesson you have learned about navigating the Finder using the new features and keyboard shortcuts. In the next lesson you'll learn about printing features in System 7.

Lesson 12
System 7
Printing

In this lesson you'll learn about improvements in printing in System 7.

What's New?

For non-LaserWriter (Apple's proprietary printer) owners, System 7 offers minor improvements in printing but no new features. If you don't own a LaserWriter or compatible printer, you may want to skip to the next lesson. System 7 does offer several new features for LaserWriter owners: constant background printing with a new Print monitoring program, enhancements to the LaserWriter driver, and a new font utility.

If you don't have a LaserWriter... Most PostScript printers can use the System 7 LaserWriter driver. The information contained in this lesson is applicable to all laser printers that can use the Apple LaserWriter driver. Check with your manufacturer if you are unsure of what driver your printer uses.

Background Printing

Background printing Background printing allows your Macintosh to send information to the printer in the background, so you don't have to wait for a document to finish printing before you can return to work.

In System 6.0.x, background printing was an option only if you ran MultiFinder. Now you can use background printing at any time. To turn background printing on:

1. Select **Chooser** from the Apple menu. The window will appear, as shown in Figure 12-1.

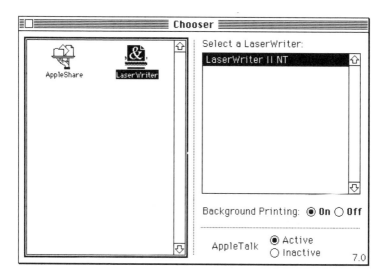

Figure 12-1. The Chooser.

2. Click on the icon of your LaserWriter at the left.

3. Click the **On** button on the right side in the Background Printing portion of the window.

LaserWriter Enhancements

The LaserWriter drivers have also been improved, giving you more control over your printing. When you select **Print** from the File menu and the LaserWriter print box comes up, you will notice two new selections at the bottom of the dialog box, Print and Destination (see Figure 12-2).

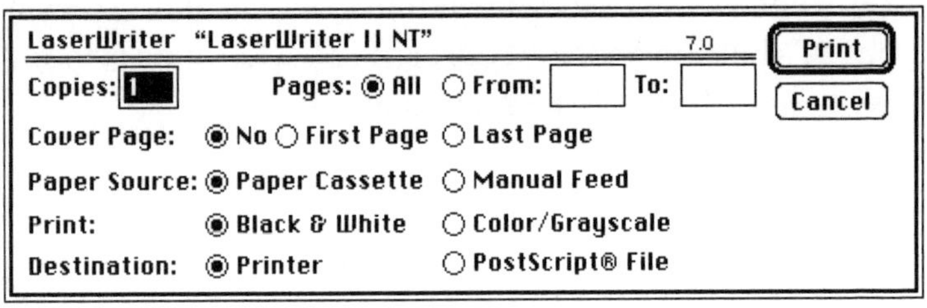

```
┌─────────────────────────────────────────────────────────────┐
│ LaserWriter  "LaserWriter II NT"              7.0  ┌─Print─┐  │
│ Copies:█          Pages: ◉ All  ○ From:     To:    ├────────┤ │
│ Cover Page:   ◉ No ○ First Page ○ Last Page        └Cancel──┘ │
│ Paper Source: ◉ Paper Cassette ○ Manual Feed                 │
│ Print:        ◉ Black & White  ○ Color/Grayscale             │
│ Destination:  ◉ Printer        ○ PostScript® File            │
└─────────────────────────────────────────────────────────────┘
```

Figure 12-2. The new LaserWriter print dialog box.

The Print option allows you to choose whether to print in color or black and white. Selecting **Black & White** will print the document with black letters on white paper—the standard way the LaserWriter has always printed. Selecting **Color** will allow you to use true color and grayscale printers and, if selected with a black-and-white LaserWriter, will simulate grays rather than printing blotchy black-and-white-only images.

Choose the Destination option to output your document to a PostScript file. A PostScript file contains the raw PostScript information in a text format. Many new programs can use this PostScript file so that you can now edit or print your documents on PostScript or even non-PostScript printers. You can also take your PostScript files to local service bureaus to print your files on their high-quality printers.

PostScript PostScript is the language used by LaserWriters and other printers. A PostScript file gives the printer specific instructions on how to lay out and print each page.

LaserWriter Font Utility (LFU)

The LaserWriter Font Utility enables LaserWriter owners to send PostScript fonts from their computer to the printer to speed up print time.

Downloading Downloading fonts is the process of sending fonts from your computer to your printer. If you have a hard disk on your printer, the fonts will stay indefinitely. If you have only memory, then you will have to download fonts every time you turn the printer off and on.

The LFU is on the Tidbits disk (or the More Tidbits disk if you use 800K floppies), which came with your System 7 upgrade. To send a PostScript font from your computer to the printer:

1. Launch the LFU from the Tidbits disk by double-clicking on its icon. The initial screen of the LaserWriter Font Utility appears.

2. Select ░ ░ ░ ░ ░ from the File menu.

3. A dialog box will open, as shown in Figure 12-3. Click on ░ ░ ░....

4. Select the fonts you want to add to the download list and choose ░ ░ ░... after each one.

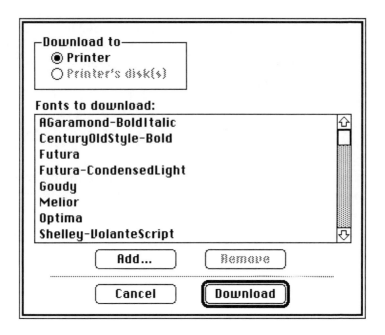

Figure 12-3. The Download Fonts dialog box from the LaserWriter Font Utility.

5. Click **Done**. The download window will reappear.

6. Click **Download**.

7. Click **OK** after the download is completed.

If you're tired of all those test pages... To stop printing the wasteful test page, choose **Start Page** from the Utilities menu and use the On and Off buttons to turn the test page on or off.

In this lesson, you have learned some of the new printing features of System 7. In the next lesson you will learn how to deal with and use the different types of fonts available to users of System 7.

Lesson 13
Fonts and System 7

In this lesson you'll learn about fonts and how to use them with System 7.

What's New?

Previous versions of the Macintosh system could deal with only two kinds of fonts, bitmap and PostScript. System 7 introduces a new font technology, TrueType, and changes the way you deal with PostScript fonts. Following is information on the installation of your fonts (more detailed information on the file types and options for dealing with your fonts appears later in this lesson).

- All of your existing bitmap fonts will be placed in the System file. Any accompanying TrueType fonts will be installed as well.

- Your PostScript fonts will be placed in the Extensions folder. You should consider conversion to TrueType if you don't have a PostScript laser printer and use a utility like Adobe Type Manager (ATM) to display PostScript fonts on-screen or if you want to display them in high quality.

71

Bitmap, PostScript, and TrueType Fonts

Following is a brief description of the three different font types:

- *Bitmap fonts*—Bitmap fonts are the fonts that your Macintosh displayed on-screen in System 6. At large or odd sizes they have jagged edges and do not print well on a LaserWriter. In System 7 you need bitmap fonts for on-screen display, but it's a good idea to have accompanying TrueType or PostScript files so the fonts print well and are displayed clearly. Bitmap fonts are stored in the System file in System 7. A bitmap font icon is shown in Figure 13-1.

Courier 12

Figure 13-1. A bitmap font icon.

- *PostScript fonts*—PostScript fonts are high quality outline fonts, which print well on laser printers. Each PostScript file contains formulas that allow you to produce the font at any size; the formulas describe the path (outline of each character) of the font. PostScript fonts (as shown in Figure 13-2) are located in the Extensions folder but need accompanying screen fonts (bitmap or TrueType) to be displayed on-screen. PostScript or high quality printers need PostScript fonts to print well.

Figure 13-2. A PostScript font icon.

- *TrueType fonts*—TrueType fonts are Apple's new font standard, introduced with System 7. These fonts combine the screen-display capabilities of bitmap fonts with the high quality smoothness of PostScript fonts. You can scale TrueType fonts to any size for high quality printing. If you have a PostScript laser printer, it's a good idea to keep accompanying PostScript fonts because they print more quickly and clearly than TrueType fonts on PostScript printers. TrueType fonts (as shown in Figure 13-3) are located in the System folder.

Figure 13-3. A TrueType font icon.

For the best screen display... Although TrueType fonts theoretically can be displayed on-screen at any size, the computer has trouble showing fonts of smaller sizes (9-24 points). It's a good idea to keep small point size bitmap fonts in the System file for each TrueType font.

System 7 Fonts and How To Get More

System 7 comes with a selection of bitmap and TrueType fonts. Chicago, Courier, Geneva, Helvetica, Monaco, New York, Times, and Symbol are provided in TrueType and bitmap forms, and they are installed with your system. The Fonts disk also contains the following fonts in bitmap form only:

- Athens

- Cairo

- London

- Los Angeles

- Palatino

- San Francisco

- Venice

You can obtain bitmap fonts almost anywhere. Many local users' groups have a collection of free or shareware bitmap fonts; for shareware fonts you send the maker a small amount of money if you like the fonts. BBSs and on-line services also have bitmap fonts, and many commercial packages are available. PostScript fonts are also available from a large number of sources commercially. You might check in a Macintosh magazine under some of the major advertisers for font information because many local stores do not carry fonts. TrueType, because it is a new format, is not yet supported widely, but expect new TrueType fonts to be available soon both commercially and publicly.

What To Do with PostScript Fonts

If you have a PostScript printer and want to have high quality display fonts, or if you don't have a PostScript printer and use a utility like Adobe Type Manager, it's a good idea to convert your PostScript fonts to TrueType. If you want to convert your fonts, there are several third party conversion programs available. See Lesson 20, "Converting Fonts to TrueType," for more information on converting your fonts.

In this lesson you have learned about the three font types of System 7 and how to obtain new fonts. The next lesson will teach you about the aliasing features of System 7.

Lesson 14
Aliases

In this lesson you'll learn about the new aliasing functions of System 7.

What Is an Alias?

Aliases are an entirely new feature of System 7. Aliases are small files that act like "remote controls" to your files and applications. When you open or launch an alias, it will open the actual file, wherever it is—even if it is on another disk or buried deep in your hard disk. Take a look at how to make an alias and at some of its uses.

Making an Alias

To make an alias of a document, file, disk, or folder:

1. In the Finder, select the file for which you want to make an alias.

2. Choose Make Alias from the File menu.

The alias will appear to the lower right of the icon for which you just made an alias. The alias is small (only a few kilobytes in file size), and its name is italicized. Aliases are always identifiable by their italicized print (see Figure 14-1).

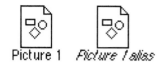

Picture 1   *Picture 1 alias*

Figure 14-1. A document and its alias.

Aliases on the Desktop

Aliases are useful for opening your applications and files. Many users make aliases of their most-used programs and documents and put them in an area on the desktop where they are easily accessible. To put an alias on the desktop:

1. Make an alias of the file you want, as shown in the preceding section.

2. Select the alias and drag it to the bottom of the desktop.

3. Rename your file (see Lesson 5, "System 7 Refinements"), and remove the *alias* from the end of the name.

Double-click on the alias whenever you want to open the program or the document it represents. A desktop with aliases on the bottom of the screen is shown in Figure 14-2.

Aliases in the Apple Menu

Aliases are also useful in the Apple menu. Just as you can open Desk Accessories or control panels by selecting them in the Apple menu, you can also open favorite files or applications using an alias. To put an alias in the Apple menu:

1. Make an alias of the file you want.

2. Select the alias and drag it onto the desktop.

3. Open the System folder.

4. Use the scroll bars to find the Apple Menu Items folder.

5. Drag the alias into the Apple Menu Items folder. The next time you open the Apple menu, the alias you added will appear in the list. Selecting the alias will open the original file.

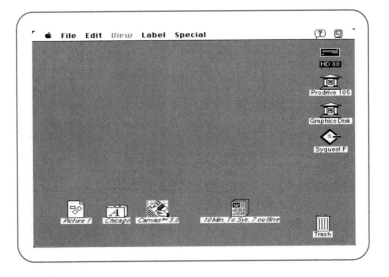

Figure 14-2. Aliases on the desktop.

Linking to Floppy Disk Files

When you work with a large number of floppy disks, you can easily forget which files are on which disks. Aliases can help you organize your floppies. You can make aliases of files that are stored on your floppy disks and copy them onto your hard drive. Then, whenever you want to open a file from a floppy disk, just open the alias as if it were a normal file and the computer will tell you which floppy disk to insert. For example, opening the alias of the Chicago font suitcase prompts you to insert the Fonts floppy disk, where the real Chicago resides, as shown in Figure 14-3.

Figure 14-3. Opening an alias of a file on a floppy disk.

The "Untitled" Syndrome It is a good idea to give meaningful names to your floppy disks. If all of your floppies are untitled, then you have no way of knowing which floppy the aliased file is located on (see "Renaming Files" in Lesson 5 for instructions on renaming).

Aliases of Network Files

On a large network, it's often time-consuming to look for files on the Server because all information must be sent over the network. If you make an alias of a file off the Server and copy it to your personal hard disk drive, then you can essentially keep all the necessary files on your own hard drive. If you treat the alias of the networked item as a normal file, the computer will automatically access the Server and find the correct file.

Other Uses for Aliases

There are unlimited uses for aliases. For example, if an item fits into your hard disk organization in several ways (that is, if a document is common to two projects that you're working on), make an alias so that you can access the file in both areas. If a folder you use often is buried deep in other folders, make an alias of it and put it on the desktop so that you can access it more easily.

In this lesson you have learned how to make aliases and how to use them. The next lesson will give you information about how System 7 deals with memory.

Lesson 15
Memory

In this lesson you'll learn about the new memory features of System 7.

Macintosh Memory Overview

In System 6 users had little control over the memory of their machine. Some memory could be used to set a *disk cache*.

> **Cache** A cache (pronounced cash) is memory set aside by your Macintosh to speed it up. This process works by loading information from your disks into memory. Because memory works faster than your disk drives, the cache speeds up your disk response times.

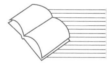

In System 6.0.x memory was also used for multitasking. (For more information on multitasking, see Lesson 10.) To use the MultiFinder effectively (the old way to multitask on a Macintosh), you had to add more memory so that you could run many programs at the same time. Also, System 6 could only access up to 8M of memory, limiting the number of programs you could run at the same time.

Megabyte A megabyte is a common measure of memory. One megabyte is approximately one million characters of information. Macintoshes come with 1, 2, 4, or 8M of memory.

System 7 solves these memory problems and limitations with a new control panel called Memory. The Memory control panel introduces a better system of caching and also enables virtual memory and 32-bit addressing. Virtual memory allows you to set aside a portion of your hard disk space as extra memory, saving you the expense of buying real memory (RAM). To use virtual memory, you need a Macintosh with a 68030 (or better) *processor*.

Processor A processor is the "engine" inside your Macintosh, which handles the bulk of the calculations your Mac performs. Macs with the 68030 processor include the SE/30, IIx, IIcx, IIci, IIsi, and the IIfx.

Macintoshes with the older 68020 processors can use virtual memory if you buy a *PMMU* chip for them. Check with your computer dealer for more information on getting a PMMU.

PMMU A PMMU (Paged Memory Management Unit) is a chip that enables you to use memory in more advanced ways, such as virtual memory (see the next section). The PMMU is built into the 68030 processor. A 68020-based Mac with a PMMU unit added is roughly equivalent in capabilities to a 68030.

System 7 also solves the problem of the 8M RAM limit set by System 6.0.x. Now if you have a 32-bit clean Macintosh, you can access hundreds of megabytes of memory (refer to the section, "32-Bit Cleanliness," for more information). 32-bit clean Macintoshes include the IIci, IIsi, and IIfx. New software and hardware enhancements, which make other 68030 Macintoshes 32-bit clean, will be introduced soon.

Virtual Memory

If you have a Macintosh with a 68030 (or 68020 with a PMMU), you can use virtual memory to enable your Macintosh to run more programs at the same time. Before you use virtual memory, your computer must meet the following conditions:

- You need enough free space on your hard drive for the total amount of memory you want to have. For example, if you have 4M of normal memory and want to add 10M of virtual memory, you must have 14M free.

- The free space in your hard disk should not be *fragmented.*

Fragmentation   Hard drives become fragmented after use. When you erase files, you leave gaps in the space on your hard disk. New files are saved in pieces to fill the gaps, but virtual memory needs a contiguous space on your hard disk. You can defragment hard disks with commercial utilities like Disk Express II or Norton Utilities.

- Your hard disk must have a current *driver.* A driver is the invisible software that allows your hard disk to work with your Macintosh. Because virtual memory uses the hard disk, some older drivers will not work with virtual memory. If you have an Apple hard disk drive, the new hard drive software comes on the Disk Tools disk.

If your computer meets these requirements, take the following steps to turn on virtual memory:

1. Select Control Panels from the Apple menu.

2. Double-click on the Memory control panel. (You may have to use the scroll bars on the bottom and right to find it). The Memory control panel will open, as shown in Figure 15-1.

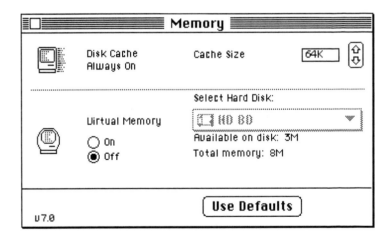

Figure 15-1. The Memory control panel.

3. Click On under the Virtual Memory portion of the window.

4. Select the hard disk you want to have the virtual memory file on by choosing it from the Select Hard Disk pop-up menu.

5. Use the small arrows on the right of the Virtual Memory part of the window to set the total memory you want to have.

   You're out of room If the arrows don't appear on the right of the Virtual Memory section, you probably don't have enough contiguous free space. Delete unnecessary files and use a defragmenter if necessary to clear the required amount of space.

6. After you set the amount of memory you want to add, close the Memory control panel and restart your computer by choosing Restart from the Special menu in the Finder.

Your Macintosh will now perform as if you have the amount of virtual memory that you specified. You can load as many applications into memory as you want (see Lesson 10, "The Applications Menu," for more information on switching between applications). Note, however, that the switching process may be slower because your "memory" is now partially on your hard disk.

32-Bit Cleanliness

Earlier in this lesson you briefly learned about the concept of being 32-bit clean. If you have a Macintosh with an older 68000 processor (Mac 512k, Plus, SE, Classic), then skip to the next section, "Disk Cache."

32-bit clean 32-bit clean Macintoshes can use large amounts of memory with System 7.

The 68020 and 68030 processors are 32-bit processors. 32-bit processors can handle larger amounts of memory than 68000 processors can. Some of the older 68020 and 68030 Macintoshes are not 32-bit clean and have a limit of 8M of memory. At the time these computers were constructed, 8M was considered more than enough for any software available. Currently, many people need large amounts of memory so that they can use more than one application at a time. Newer Macs, such as the LC, IIci, IIsi, and IIfx, are 32-bit clean and with System 7 can use over 100M of memory.

There are, however, some methods that might make older Macintoshes 32-bit clean. Third party utilities as well as new *ROM*s are in development to make these older Macs 32-bit clean. For now, you must stay with the 8M memory limit if you have one of these Macs.

ROM ROM is an acronym for Read Only Memory. ROMs contain vital information for the Macintosh interface and how the system software deals with the hardware (chips, etc.). Unlike RAM, the information stored in ROM is not lost when you turn off the Mac.

To turn on 32-bit mode on 32-bit clean machines:

1. Select **Control Panels** from the Apple menu.

2. Open the Memory control panel. (You may have to use the scroll bars on the bottom and right to find it.)

3. Click **On** under 32-Bit Addressing.

4. Close the Memory control panel.

5. Restart your computer by choosing Restart from the Special menu in the Finder.

Disk Cache

The disk cache has not changed much from System 6. The only change is that the cache is always on. Having the cache on doesn't make much difference because a small disk cache (less than 100K) makes little speed or memory difference. Large disk caches make disk access faster but take memory away from your applications. To change the size of your disk cache to speed access on your Macintosh:

1. Select Control Panels from the Apple menu.

2. Open the Memory control panel. (You may have to use the scroll bars.)

3. Use the small arrows to the right of the Disk Cache portion of the Memory control panel to set the amount of memory you want to allocate for the disk cache (1024K=1M).

4. Close the Memory control panel.

5. Restart your computer by choosing Restart from the Special menu in the Finder. When you restart your Mac, the amount of memory you specified will be set aside as a cache and will speed repeated disk access.

In this lesson you have learned how to work with memory in System 7. The next lesson will teach you about some of the new networking features of the system.

Lesson 16
Networking

In this lesson you'll learn about the new networking
features of System 7.

What is Networking?

Networking is the connection of two or more computers
through cables that allow the computers to transfer information. Networking enables you to share files with other
computers on the network and also lets you use one shared
printer for an entire group. If you work in an office with
multiple Macintoshes, you are probably on a network. If
you're not sure, check with a computer technician.

One drawback of System 6 networking was the neces-
sity of a dedicated computer, called a File Server, just for
sharing files. With the addition of built-in file sharing
capabilities in System 7, you no longer need a dedicated
computer to share files on a network. Now every Macintosh
on a network equipped with System 7 can allow other
computers to access its files while the user is working on the
computer normally. System 6 users can access another
computer running System 7 with file sharing but cannot
allow others to use their files. This allows easier transfer of
information and frees up another computer for productive
work.

Connecting to an Existing Network

If your Mac is already connected to a network, you can access the Network File Server through the Chooser DA. To connect to an existing AppleTalk Network File Server or to access files from another file-sharing computer, follow these steps:

1. Select **Chooser** from the Apple menu.

2. Click on the AppleShare icon.

3. Click **Active** on the AppleTalk button in the lower right corner of the window. Then select **OK** when the dialog box appears.

4. A list of File Servers will appear on the right side of the window. Select the File Server you want to receive files from (see Figure 16-1).

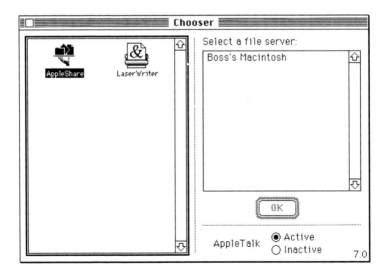

Figure 16-1. Chooser dialog box with AppleShare selected.

5. Choose the O K button.

6. A dialog box will appear, similar to the one shown in Figure 16-2. Click on **Registered User.**

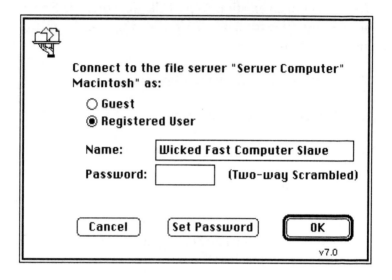

Connect to the file server "Server Computer"
Macintosh" as:

○ Guest
⦿ Registered User

Name: ⎢Wicked Fast Computer Slave⎥

Password: ⎢_____⎥ (Two-way Scrambled)

⎢ Cancel ⎥   ⎢ Set Password ⎥   ⎢ OK ⎥

v7.0

Figure 16-2. Connecting to the File Server.

7. Enter your name and password and then click O K.

Access not allowed If you aren't allowed to access the Server, a dialog box will appear telling you that your name or your password cannot be recognized. You should then check with the network administrator or user of the machine that you are trying to access.

8. Choose which drives you want to access by holding down the Shift key and clicking on the name of each drive.

9. Close the Chooser, and the drives will appear on your desktop. (You may need to restart if you chose more than one drive over the network.)

Setting Up File Sharing

System 7 allows other users on the network to access your hard disk. To set up file sharing, follow these steps:

1. Select Control Panels from the Apple menu.

2. Double-click on the Sharing Setup control panel. The control panel will open, as shown in Figure 16-3.

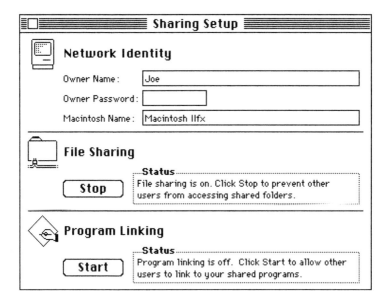

Figure 16-3. The Sharing Setup control panel.

3. Type your name, a password, and a name for your Macintosh that will be used over the network.

4. Click on the $\mathtt{Start}$ button to start file sharing.

Now, file sharing has been activated. It will take a short period of time to set itself up on the network, so wait until the $\mathtt{Status}$ in the Sharing Setup control panel is on.

To set individual hard disk drives to allow others access, follow these steps:

1. Close the Sharing Setup control panel.

2. In the Finder, select the hard disk drive you want other network users to access.

3. Select $\mathtt{Sharing}$ from the File menu.

4. A window will appear, as shown in Figure 16-4. Click on the box labeled $\mathtt{Share\ this\ item\ and\ its\ contents}$.

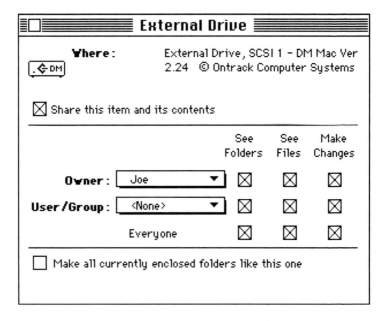

Figure 16-4. The Sharing window in the Finder.

5. Select **See Folders, See Files,** and **Make Changes** under the Everyone portion of the window. This will allow everyone on the network to access your hard disk.

   Privacy If you don't want everyone to have access to your hard disk, see the next section, "Users and Groups."

6. Close the window, and click on **Save Changes** when the dialog box comes up.

   Repeat steps 1-6 for every hard disk on your computer that you want to share.

Users and Groups

If you want different users and groups to have access to different parts of your computer, you can use the Users & Groups control panel to name specific people you'll allow to access your hard disk. To add a new user who can access your hard disk:

1. Select **Control Panels** from the Apple menu.

2. Open the Users & Groups control panel. The window will open, as shown in Figure 16-5.

3. Choose **New User** from the File menu, and type the user's name.

4. Double-click on the new user's icon. A window will open, as shown in Figure 16-6.

5. Click on the options you want this user to be able to use.

6. Close the window.

7. Click **OK** when the Save Changes dialog appears. **93**

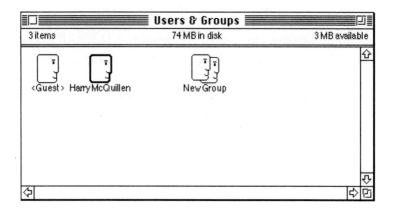

Figure 16-5. The Users & Groups control panel.

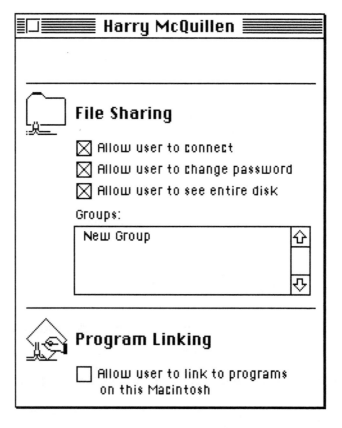

Figure 16-6. The Users & Groups window for user
Harry McQuillen.

You also can allow access for a group of people and set their access rights as a group. This feature is useful if you are working with a specific group on a certain project or if you want people from only your department to use your hard disk. To create access for a group, first add each individual as outlined in the preceding steps and then follow these additional steps:

1. Select Control Panels from the Apple menu.

2. Open the Users & Groups control panel. The window will open (see Figure 16-5 again).

3. Choose New Group from the File menu.

4. Add users to the new group by dragging their icons to the group icon and releasing.

You can give access to individual users and groups by selecting Sharing in the Finder, as discussed in the preceding section. To change the access of users or groups, select the appropriate icons from the scrolling lists and set their access rather than change the access for everyone.

In this lesson you have learned how to connect to a network and how to use System 7's new file-sharing features. In the next lesson you will learn about the new desktop in System 7.

Lesson 17
The New Desktop

In this lesson you'll learn about the new role of the desktop in System 7.

What's New?

In System 6 the desktop (Finder) on your Mac was similar to your real desktop but with icons, windows, and applications on it rather than traditional books and papers. In the Finder, the disks, Trash, and opened windows were on the desktop, and applications displayed their windows on the desktop.

System 7 uses the desktop in the same way but also adds to its usefulness. In System 7 the desktop is not only the workspace in the background, but it is also the center of the *filing system* (see Figures 17-1 and 17-2).

The desktop is now the *top level* in open and save dialogs. In Figure 17-1, for example, a dialog box shows the desktop as the top level, almost as if one large folder holds every disk and item on the desktop. In the dialog box you can see all of the disks and items on the desktop. To change between disks in System 6 you had to click the Disk button. In System 7 use the following steps to choose the disk you want to open or save something on.

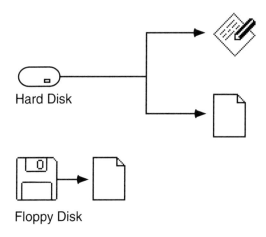

Figure 17-1. The old filing system.

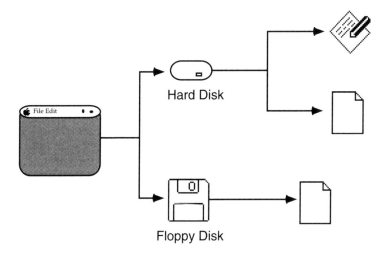

Figure 17-2. The new filing system.

Top level The top level, or root directory, is like a large folder that holds all of the contents of your disk. In System 6 the disk was the top level; in System 7 the desktop is the top level.

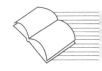

97

1. Select **Open** or **Save** from the File menu in your application.

2. When the dialog box comes up, click **Desktop** (see Figure 17-3).

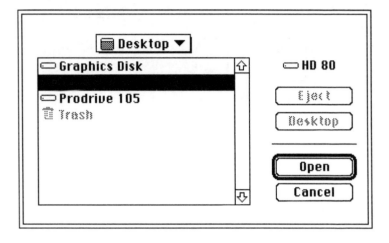

Figure 17-3. The desktop in an Open/Save dialog box.

3. The dialog box will automatically go to the desktop level (the root directory), and you will see your disks and the Trash. Double-click on the disk you want.

4. Then the dialog box works exactly like it did in System 6. Double-click or use the **Open** button just like you did in System 6 to open folders, and click in the **Open** or **Save** box to open or save your document.

Storing Files on the Desktop

It's often useful to put a file directly on the desktop in System 7 if you want easy access to it or if you're not sure where it will go in the organization of your hard disk drive. If you're in the Finder, follow these steps to place a file or an application on the desktop:

1. Make sure that the portion of the desktop you want to move the file onto is clear (that is, there are no windows hiding it). Move any windows out of the way.

2. Open your hard disk icon and folders until you open the window where your file or application is located.

3. Click on the file and drag it to the open portion of the desktop where you want to put it. Most users place icons on the bottom of the screen because the disk icons go on the right, and the top and left are often taken up by windows.

   If your desktop gets cluttered... If you want to put a file that you've placed on the desktop back in its original folder, select it and choose Put Away from the File menu.

If you're working with a file and want to save it directly to the desktop, follow these steps:

1. Select Save As... or Save from the File menu in your application.

2. Click on the Desktop button in the dialog box.

3. Type the name of your file as you want to save it.

4. Click on **saue**. Then the file will be placed on your desktop.

New Desktop Files

Even though you can't see it working, the Finder creates files on your hard disk called *desktop files*. System 6 also created these files. They store information about your disks and how to display them and their contents on your desktop. System 7 changes the desktop file format and adds two new desktop files. Most users have no need for these files, but many utilities use them. If you use a defragmentation program (discussed in Lesson 15), file recovery program (like Norton Utilities or SUM II), or other utility that looks into your hard disk to find information about your files, there's a good chance they won't work in System 7. Check with your manufacturer for information about a new version of these programs.

In this lesson you have learned about the new role of the desktop in System 7. In the next lesson you will learn about the new stationery feature.

Lesson 18
Stationery

In this lesson you'll learn about the new Stationery feature of System 7.

What is Stationery?

In everyday work situations, your stationery normally contains your letterhead. On your Macintosh you probably use some standard form for different documents. For example, your word processing documents have a standard header or footer, or your drawing program documents might have your logo put in the corner. With System 6 you had to have a document with this information, duplicate it, rename it, and then open it. System 7 makes this whole process easier by providing a stationery feature, which enables you to have common blank documents for all your applications. You can make a document called a *stationery pad*, which will automatically put your information into a blank document when you open it (see Figure 18-1).

Figure 18-1. A stationery pad icon.

The uses for stationery are unlimited. Following are only a few suggestions:

- Make a stationery pad of your letterhead for all word processing documents.

- Put your name and company logo in a stationery pad for all of your draw documents.

- Put all of your modem settings in a stationery pad for your telecommunications document.

- Make a stationery pad of forms for your database.

- Make a stationery pad with all the formulas for your monthly accounting data for your spreadsheet.

Using Stationery with New Applications

Newer applications or those updated for use with System 7 have the stationery feature built in. To make a stationery pad, follow these steps:

1. Create a stationery pad as if you are creating a normal document (check your applications manual for more information on how to create a document). Be sure to include information you'd like to have in all documents of this type.

2. Select **save** from the File menu. A dialog box will come up, as shown in Figure 18-2. Note that every application has a slightly different Save dialog box.

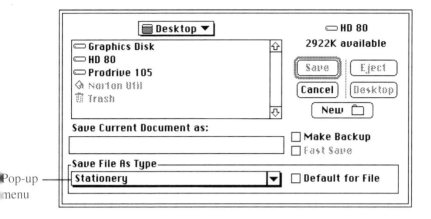

Figure 18-2. A Save dialog box of an application with the stationery feature implemented.

3. Type the name of the stationery pad. It's often helpful to include the letters **SP** or **Stationery** in the file name so you can distinguish a stationery pad from other documents.

4. Select **Stationery** from the Save File As Type pop-up menu. Some applications may have a different method for choosing file types, so consult your manual.

If you're unable to save... If your application doesn't have a Save File As Type... or similar menu or button, or if there is no option for saving as a stationery pad, skip to the next section of this lesson.

5. Click on the **Save** button.

Then you will have a stationery pad with the information you've just entered in it. When you open this document, your application will bring up a new, untitled document with this information, leaving the original file untouched.

Using Stationery with Older Applications

If your application doesn't have an option for saving to stationery, you can still use this feature. Just follow these steps to create a stationery pad:

1. Create stationery pad as if creating a normal document. Be sure to include information you'd like to have in all documents of this type.

2. Select S a υ e from the File menu.

3. Type the name of the stationery pad.

4. Click on the S a υ e button.

5. Go to the Finder. Open any necessary folders until the document you just saved is visible.

6. Click on the document icon and choose G e t I n f o from the File menu. The Get Info window will open, as shown in Figure 18-3.

7. Click on the S t a t i o n e r y P a d box.

Now, you have created a stationery pad. To create a new document with the contents of a stationery pad, follow these steps:

1. Double-click on the document icon in the Finder. A dialog box will open, as shown in Figure 18-4.

2. Type the name of the new file in which you want to have the stationery pad contents.

3. Select O K. The new document will open in your application.

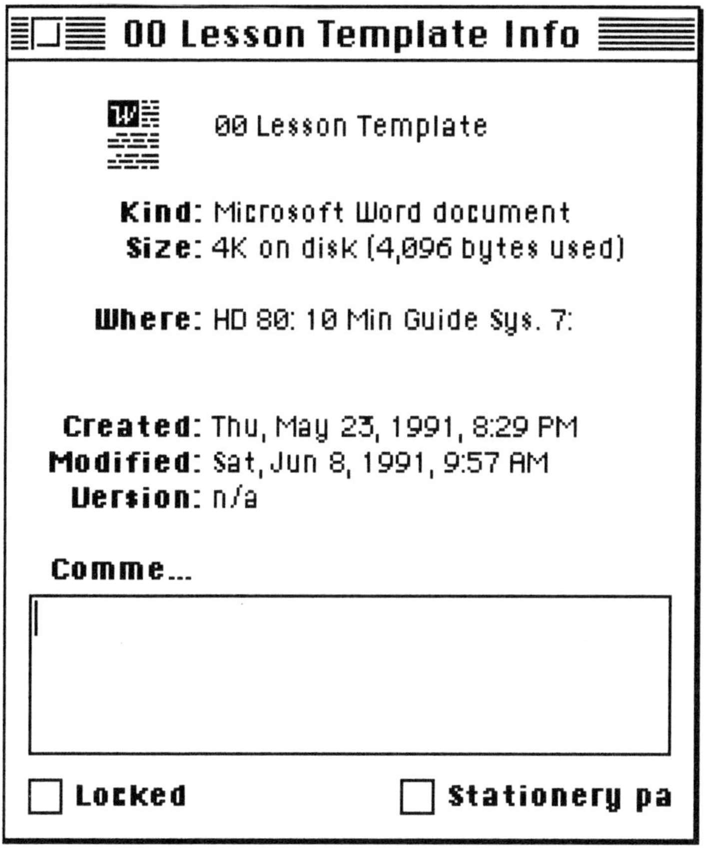

00 Lesson Template Info

00 Lesson Template

Kind: Microsoft Word document
Size: 4K on disk (4,096 bytes used)

Where: HD 80: 10 Min Guide Sys. 7:

Created: Thu, May 23, 1991, 8:29 PM
Modified: Sat, Jun 8, 1991, 9:57 AM
Version: n/a

Comme...

☐ **Locked**   ☐ **Stationery pa**

Figure 18-3. Information on a document.

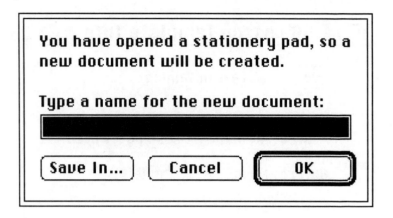

Figure 18-4. Opening a stationery pad from the Finder.

In this lesson you have learned about the new stationery pad feature of System 7. Next, you will learn about Publish and Subscribe, the inter-application communication features of System 7.

Lesson 19
Publish and Subscribe

In this lesson you'll learn about Publish and Subscribe, the new inter-application communication features of System 7.

What Is Inter-Application Communication?

While the name *Inter-Application Communication* (IAC) may sound imposing, it is a procedure very similar to the basic cut and paste functions that you've used since you first started working on a Macintosh. When you cut a diagram from your draw program and paste it into the report in your desktop publishing program, the information is transferred between the two programs. System 7 enhances this feature with a new system of inter-application communication called Publish and Subscribe. With Publish and Subscribe, your application can actively exchange information.

> **In the future...** Other forms of inter-application communication currently exist in System 7 and will be used in future products.

You can compare Publish and Subscribe to an expanded cut and paste operation. When you publish a chart from your spreadsheet, for example, you create a small file called an *edition* on your disk. Then you can go into your word processor and subscribe to this edition. The graphic will appear just as if you had pasted it. The difference from cut and paste is that when you change the numbers in your chart in the spreadsheet, you can automatically update the graph in the word processor without having to paste in the updated version or even having the word processor in your computer's memory. The Publish and Subscribe feature becomes even more helpful when this chart has been subscribed to by many documents so that every instance can be updated in one time-saving step.

Creating Editions

Creating editions is the process of publishing an item. Most new versions of applications contain or will contain the Publish and Subscribe capability. The documentation or packaging indicate whether your application has the capability to use this feature. Follow these instructions to publish:

1. Select the piece of text or graphic you want to publish in your application.

2. Choose **Create Publisher** from the Edit menu (see Figure 19-1).

3. A new window will appear, like the one shown in Figure 19-2. On the left side will be a Preview of your selection. Enter the name of the edition you want to create in the text field at the bottom of the dialog box.

Edit	
Undo	⌘Z
Cut	⌘H
Copy	⌘C
Paste	⌘U
Clear	
Create Publisher...	
Subscribe To...	
Publisher Options	
Show Clipboard	

Figure 19-1. The Edit menu of an application with Publish and Subscribe.

Incompatible applications If the Create Publisher... option (or something similar) is not in your Edit menu, then your application is probably not compatible with Publish and Subscribe. Contact the developer for a newer version if you want to use Publish and Subscribe.

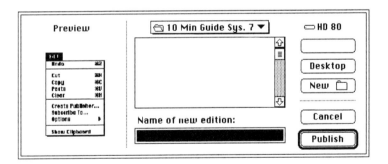

Figure 19-2. The Edition Save dialog box.

Edition The edition is the small file created for each item published that serves as a link between the Publisher and the Subscriber.

4. Select **P u b l i s h** and the selected item will be published, creating a small edition file on the disk (see Figure 19-3). Note that some applications may have custom icons for their edition files.

Figure 19-3. The generic edition icon.

The published item will be surrounded by a light gray box. You can subscribe to this edition in any capable program, and it will be pasted in. Subscribed items are surrounded by a dark gray box (see the next section).

Subscribing

Subscribing is the process of pasting an edition file into your application. To subscribe to an item:

1. Position your selection arrow where you want the information from the edition inserted (this may differ from application to application).

2. Select **S u b s c r i b e T o . . .** from the Edit menu. The dialog box will open, as shown in Figure 19-4. Depending on the application, the dialog box may list only the editions or it may list other files as well.

3. Choose the edition you want to subscribe to. When you choose an edition, a preview of it will appear on the right side of the dialog box.

4. Click on **S u b s c r i b e**. The item will then be pasted in and will appear in a dark gray box (see Figure 19-5).

Figure 19-4. A sample Subscribe To... dialog box.

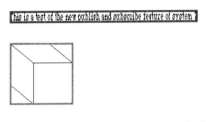

Figure 19-5. Subscribed text surrounded by a dark box and a published cube surrounded by a light gray box.

Updating Files

The capability of Publish and Subscribe to update is one of its more useful features. After you have changed the original item and want to update every file it has subscribed to, use the following steps:

1. Open the application you used to create the item that you want to change, and make the necessary changes to the published item (for example, a spreadsheet containing your monthly budget).

2. Select the published item (the spreadsheet for this exercise).

3. Choose **Publisher Options** from the File menu.

4. A dialog box will open, as shown in Figure 19-6. Choose whether you want to update the subscribers *on save* or *manually*. On Save means that whenever the document is saved, all subscribers will be updated. Manually requires that you select **Send Edition Now** every time you want to update. For this exercise, click on **Send Edition Now**.

All subscribers will be updated, and every subscribed instance of the spreadsheet will be changed.

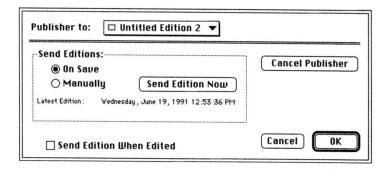

Figure 19-6. A Publisher Options dialog box.

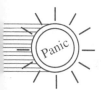

Where is the Publisher Options dialog box? Some applications may handle the update process differently. If there is no Publisher Options dialog box or menu selection, check your application manual.

In this lesson you have learned about the Publish and Subscribe features of System 7. The next lesson will teach you how to convert your PostScript fonts to TrueType.

Lesson 20
Converting Fonts to TrueType

In this lesson you'll learn how to convert your PostScript fonts to the TrueType format.

Why Convert Your Fonts?

There are several reasons why you might want to convert your PostScript fonts to TrueType fonts. For example, if you have a PostScript printer, you might want to convert your PostScript fonts to TrueType so you can take advantage of the way TrueType fonts are displayed on-screen. (TrueType fonts are outline fonts and do not have jagged edges, even at large or nonstandard sizes. For more information, see Lesson 13, "Fonts and System 7.") If you use ATM (Adobe Type Manager) to print PostScript fonts with a non-PostScript printer and display items on-screen, it's simpler to use TrueType fonts than the sometimes inconvenient ATM setup.

 If you don't want to convert... You do not have to convert your PostScript fonts to the TrueType format. If you are satisfied with your current fonts, you can continue using them with no modifications.

What To Use To Convert Your Fonts

If you want to convert your PostScript fonts to TrueType fonts, you currently have two main options. Metamorphosis Pro 2.0 gives you basic font conversion capability, but FontMonger is easier to use and slightly quicker than Metamorphosis. FontMonger is used in this lesson. You can get this program from your local software store or from one of the large mail order companies.

How To Convert Fonts

To convert your fonts using FontMonger, follow these steps:

1. Copy the contents of your original PostScript font disks into a new folder on your hard disk. You should have one suitcase file and several font files (see Figure 20-1).

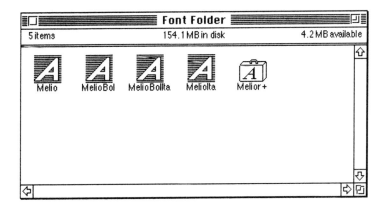

Figure 20-1. A suitcase and several PostScript fonts.

2. Double-click on the FontMonger icon to launch the application. A dialog box will appear with the FontMonger information, and the screen will then clear.

3. Select **Convert Batch** from the File menu.

4. The dialog box will open, as shown in Figure 20-2. Click on the **Drive** button until the hard disk where your fonts are stored is shown in the upper right corner of the screen.

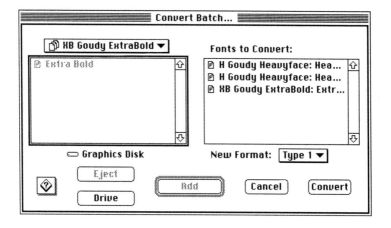

Figure 20-2. The main dialog box of FontMonger.

5. Open the folder where the font you want to convert is stored. Select the suitcase and click on **Open**.

6. The suitcase will open and on the left portion of the window will display the names of the fonts contained in it. Select the font you want to work with and click on **Open**.

7. The list of variations of the font (that is, bold, italic) will appear in the left side of the window. Hold down the Shift key, select the variations you want to convert, and click on ᴀ ᴅ ᴅ.

8. Repeat this process until the Fonts to Convert: list contains all of the fonts you want to convert.

9. Select ᴛ ʀ ᴜ ᴇ ᴛ ʏ ᴘ ᴇ from the New Format menu under the Fonts to Convert: list.

10. Click on ᴄ ᴏ ɴ ᴠ ᴇ ʀ ᴛ.

11. A dialog box will open, as shown in Figure 20-3. Click on ᴏ ʀ ɪ ɢ ɪ ɴ ᴀ ʟ to save your converted fonts under the same name as your old fonts.

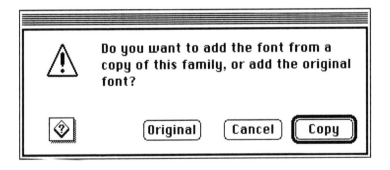

Figure 20-3. A FontMonger dialog box.

Another dialog box will come up, informing you of the status of the conversion. Don't worry if the conversion seems to take a long time, most font conversions take a while. There is also an option for canceling the conversion. Your original fonts will remain in the Extensions folder. These TrueType fonts will replace only the fonts copied from the disk.

Now, your fonts have been converted. Your suitcases will contain the proper TrueType fonts, as well as all needed bitmaps. To install these fonts, use the procedures for installing fonts outlined in Lesson 6, "The New System Folder." If you have a PostScript laser printer, make sure that your original PostScript fonts are still in the Extensions folder. If not, be sure to copy any PostScript fonts back into your Extensions folder from the original disks.

The process for using Metamorphosis Pro is slightly different, so refer to your manual before converting fonts with this program.

With this lesson you have finished the *10 Minute Guide to System 7*. Following this lesson you will find a "System Software Primer," which will give you some basic definitions of the system software pieces and the basic Macintosh mouse and keyboard operations.

Overtime

System Software Primer

If you don't know how to use a Macintosh well or if you haven't used one recently, the "System Software Primer" contains basic information about the system software and basic Macintosh operations.

Basic Macintosh Operations

The Macintosh interface is consistent with menus at the top of the screen and the desktop, and all dialog boxes and windows operate in a similar fashion. First, look at some of the basic ways you use to operate your Macintosh. The following operations are used throughout the Mac environment in the Finder and through applications.

Button-Click   To click on a button, move your mouse pointer (arrow) into the middle of the button and then click the mouse button once.

Menu selection   To select an item from a menu, move your mouse so the pointer is over the name of the menu and hold down the mouse

	button. The menu will pop open. Drag the pointer down the list of menu items. When the pointer is over the item you want to select, release the button.
Double-click	To double-click to open an application, folder, or file from a dialog box or the Finder, move the mouse pointer over the icon of the item you want to choose, and then press the mouse button two times in close succession.
Select	To select an item in the Finder or in a dialog box, move the mouse pointer over the icon of the item and click once until the color changes to black (or other dark color on color Macs).
Drag	To drag an icon in the Finder (to move, copy, or trash it), select the icon, move your mouse pointer to the selected icon, and then press and hold the mouse button. While holding the button, move your mouse pointer (an outline of the icon will follow) to where you want to place the item and then release the button.
Shift-click	To select more than one item in the Finder or in some dialog boxes, hold down the Shift key and select each item you want.

Typing and Selecting Text

Typing text on a Macintosh is similar to typing text on any computer or typewriter. Most applications have an option for typing text. There is no need to enter a Return at the end of a line unless you are done with a paragraph because the Mac automatically scrolls to the next line.

To select text for copying or pasting, move the mouse to the beginning of the text you want to select. Press and hold the mouse button, and then release the button when you have moved the pointer to the end of the text.

System Software Overview

You need system software to use your Macintosh; it provides the necessary information to your computer to allow it to run programs and present you with the Macintosh interface of windows, icons, and the desktop.

The desktop (also known as the Finder) on your Mac is similar to your real desktop but with icons, windows, and applications on it rather than traditional books and papers (see Figure A.1). The desktop is the "background" of your Macintosh screen and is normally a light gray color. (You can customize the color and pattern of the desktop.) In the Finder, the disks, Trash, and opened windows are on the desktop, and applications display their windows on the desktop also. At the top of the desktop screen is a menu bar, which has the Apple menu on the far left and your Application menus in the middle. System 7 also places the Balloon Help and Applications menus on the right of the menu bar.

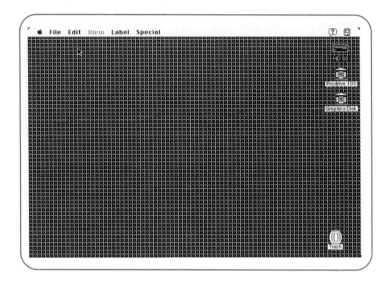

Figure A-1. The basic desktop.

The system software resides in a folder on your hard disk. It's a good idea to know what is in your System folder so that you can add or remove items to customize your Mac for your particular use (that is, adding fonts, DAs, etc.). Following is a list of items that reside in your System folder:

- *System file*—Contains basic information that your Mac needs to run and contains fonts.

- *Finder*—Makes the desktop and provides file launching and manipulation capabilities.

- *Desk Accessories*—Small applications like the Calculator and Notepad, which you can use to replace some of the items lying on your real desktop.

- *INITs*—INITs from System 6 are called Startup documents in System 7. INITs are small utilities that load into your computer's memory at startup and make your Mac more productive and easier to use.

- *CDEVs*—CDEVs from System 6 are called control panels in System 7. CDEVs allow you to control various parts of your Macintosh and fine-tune utilities and other items.

- *Preferences*—Files created by your applications. They contain information on how you like your program set up (such as default page size, which fonts you use, or how your menus are configured).

- *Printer Drivers*—Software needed to use your printer.

Index

G

H

I

K

L

M